D0181420

NOLS
Wilderness Wisdom

Quotes for Inspirational Exploration

edited by John Gookin

STACKPOLE
BOOKS

0 11557 02646 7

Copyright © 2003 by The National Outdoor Leadership School

Published by
STACKPOLE BOOKS
5067 Ritter Road
Mechanicsburg, PA 17055
www.stackpolebooks.com

All rights reserved, including the right to reproduce this book or portions thereof in any form or by any means, electronic or mechanical, including photocopying, recording, or by any information storage and retrieval system, without permission in writing from the publisher. All inquiries should be addressed to Stackpole Books, 5067 Ritter Road, Mechanicsburg, Pennsylvania 17055.

Printed in the United States of America

10 9 8 7 6 5 4 3 2 1

First edition

Cover design by Caroline Stover
Cover photograph by Tom Bol

Library of Congress Cataloging-in-Publication Data

Wilderness wisdom : edited by John Gookin.
    p. cm.
Includes index.
  ISBN 0-8117-2646-0
  1. Nature—Quotations, maxims, etc. 2. Outdoor life—Quotations, maxims, etc. I. Gookin, John.
  PN6084.N2 W55 2003
  796.5—dc21

                                                    2002010835

Contents

Wisdom seems more compelling when expressed in a quote.
Well-chosen words give structure to an entire chain of experiences.
There is education and comfort in the notion that others have already
navigated life's turbulent waters.

Andy Dappen

Introduction

The readings in this book are organized to reflect the curriculum, values, and mission of the National Outdoor Leadership School, and have been compiled from the collections of various instructors over several decades. Currently NOLS has nearly 700 instructors and over 60,000 alumni throughout the world. Together they form a diverse and spirited group of individuals. While each uses readings in a variety of ways, here are some general thoughts that may help you to best use this book.

A good quote helps us to better understand our life experiences. While we may feel an intuitive appreciation for an experience, a quote that precisely articulates what we are feeling allows us to view the experience in a new light. We see the bigger picture. With this increased awareness we can take our initial feelings and turn them into a philosophy of life.

Finding this kind of inspiration in quotes is a personal process. Some will ring true for you; others won't. It is up to each of us to find our own inspiration in life's events. Use the thoughts that resonate for you in order to define the life that you desire.

If a quote inspires you, use it carefully with others. With old friends we may be able to blurt some quote out and have it appreciated. With recent acquaintances, we should be more cautious by saying that the reading is one that inspired us, and that we would like to share it. We don't need to apologize for how we feel about the idea, but it would be insensitive of us to expect others to always share our feelings.

As we have collected the quotes in this book we have used them not just as a path to individual inspiration but also as a means of group discussion. By provoking thought and encouraging conversation with others, these readings have helped us to discuss important ethical questions and the values we share as a community.

Building this collection was a team effort. Thank you to Mike Clelland, Jeff Louden, Heather MacLeod, Aimee Hoyt, Willie Williams, Jim Chisholm, Morgan Hite, and others for both their contributions and their sage advice.

Beauty

Beauty—the adjustment of all parts proportionately so that one cannot add or subtract or change without impairing the harmony of the whole.

Leon Battista Alberti

Far away in the sunshine are my highest inspirations. I may not read them, but I can look up and see the beauty, believe in them and try to follow where they lead.

Louisa May Alcott

All beauty has some strangeness of proportion.

Francis Bacon

That wonderful world of high mountains, dazzling in their rock and ice, acts as a catalyst. It suggests the infinite but it is not the infinite. The heights only give us what we ourselves bring them.

Lucien Devies

Though we travel the world over to find the beautiful, we must carry it with us or we find it not.

Ralph Waldo Emerson

To the attentive eye, each moment of the year has its own beauty, and in the same field, it beholds, every hour, a picture which was never seen before, and which shall never be seen again.

Ralph Waldo Emerson
Nature

The hours when the mind is absorbed by beauty are the only hours when we truly live.

Richard Jefferies

Beauty is an ecstasy; it is as simple as hunger. There is really nothing to be said about it.

W. Somerset Maugham

These beautiful days must enrich all my life. They do not exist as mere pictures—maps hung upon the walls of memory—but they saturate themselves into every part of my body and live always.

John Muir

Beauty is composed of many things and never stands alone. It is part of horizons, blue in the distance, great primeval silences, knowledge of all things on earth. . . . It is so fragile it can be destroyed by a sound or a thought. It may be infinitesimally small or encompass the universe itself. It comes in a swift conception wherever nature has not been disturbed.

Sigurd Olson

The heavens declare God's glory and the magnificence of what made them. Each new dawn is a miracle; each new sky fills with beauty. Their testimony speaks to the whole world and reaches to the ends of the earth. In them is a path for the sun, who steps forth handsome as a bridegroom and rejoices like an athlete as he runs. He starts at one end of the heavens and circles to the other end, and nothing can hide from his heat.

Psalms 19:1–6

I am roaring drunk with the lust of life and adventure and unbearable beauty.

Everett Ruess

Biodiversity

The swift metamorphosis and the onward march of civilization, sweeping ever westward and transforming and taming our wilderness, fills us with a strange regret, and we rejoice that parts of that wilderness will yet remain to us unchanged.

William S. Bracket

Diversity, be it ever so little, has value in relieving stress.

Frank Fraser Darling

When a community or species has no known worth or other economic value to humanity, it is as dishonest and unwise to trump up weak resource values for it as it is unnecessary to abandon the effort to conserve it.

David Ehrenfeld
The Arrogance of Humanism

We consider species to be like a brick in the foundation of a building. You can probably lose one or two or a dozen bricks and still have a standing house. But by the time you've lost twenty percent of species, you're going to destabilize the entire structure. That's the way ecosystems work.

Donald Falk
The Christian Science Monitor, May 26, 1989

The links between ecosystem and human health are many and obvious: the value in wetlands of filtering pollutants out of groundwater aquifers; the potential future medical use of different plants' genetic material; the human health effects of heavy metal accumulation in fish and shellfish. It is clear that healthy ecosystems provide the underpinnings for the long-term health of economies and societies.

F. Henry Habicht, former Deputy Administrator, EPA

Natural species are the library from which genetic engineers can work.

Thomas E. Lovejoy

In our concern for the whooping crane we are at once symbolizing and concealing a far deeper anxiety—namely, the prospective total extermination of all species.

Lewis Mumford
The Future Environments of America

Without knowing it, we utilize hundreds of products each day that owe their origin to wild animals and plants. Indeed our welfare is intimately tied up with the welfare of wildlife. Well may conservationists proclaim that by saving the lives of wild species, we may be saving our own.

Norman Myers

The habitat of an organism is the place where it lives, or the place where one would go to find it. The ecological niche, on the other hand, is the position or status of an organism within its community and ecosystem resulting from the organism's structural adaptations, physiological responses and specific behavior (inherited and/or learned). The ecological niche of an organism depends not only on where it lives, but also on what it does. By analogy, it may be said that the habitat is the organism's "address," and the niche is its "profession," biologically speaking.

William E. Odum
Fundamentals of Ecology

Relatively few benefits have flowed to the people who live closest to the more than 3,000 protected areas that have been established in tropical countries during the past 50 years. For this reason, the preservation of biodiversity is often thought of as something that poor people are asked to do to fulfill the wishes of rich people living in comfort thousands of miles away.

Peter H. Raven

The coastal zone may be the single most important portion of our planet. The loss of its biodiversity may have repercussions far beyond our worst fears.

G. Carleton Ray
Biodiversity

Why do they prefer to tell stories about the possible medicinal benefits of the Houston toad rather than to offer moral reasons for supporting the Endangered Species Act? That law is plainly ideological; it is hardly to be excused on economic grounds.

Mark Sagoff

Thus, remarkably, we do not know the true number of species on earth even to the nearest order of magnitude. My own guess, based on the described fauna and flora and many discussions with entomologists and other specialists, is that the absolute number falls somewhere between five and thirty million.

Edward O. Wilson
Conservation for the 21st Century

Character

A person may be qualified to do greater good to humankind and become more beneficial to the world, by morality without faith than by faith without morality.

Joseph Addison

A cloudy day, or a little sunshine, have as great an influence on many constitutions as the most sacred blessings or misfortunes.

Joseph Addison

We are what we consistently do. Excellence is defined by our habits.

Aristotle

Modesty is hardly to be described as a virtue. It is a feeling rather than a disposition. It is a kind of fear of falling into disrepute.

Aristotle

Never let your sense of morals prevent you from doing what is right.

Isaac Asimov

Polish doesn't change quartz into a diamond.

Wilma Askinas

The Eskimo has fifty-two names for snow because it is important to them; there ought to be as many for love.

Margaret Atwood

Character builds slowly, but it can be torn down with incredible swiftness.

Faith Baldwin

Climbing is not a battle with the elements, nor against the law of gravity. It's a battle against oneself.

Walter Bonatti

Our character is what we do when we think no one is looking.

H. Jackson Browne

What is liberty without wisdom and without virtue?

Edmund Burke

The great hope of society is individual character.

William Ellery Channing

The nobler sort of man emphasizes the good qualities in others, and does not accentuate the bad.

Confucius

A man does not climb a mountain without bringing some of it away with him and leaving something of himself upon it.

Martin Conway

The ideals which have always shone before me and filled me with the joy of living are goodness, beauty, and truth. To make a goal of comfort or happiness has never appealed to me; a system of ethics built on this basis would be sufficient only for a herd of cattle.

Albert Einstein

What you do speaks so loudly that I cannot hear what you say.
Ralph Waldo Emerson

Keep company with those who make you better.

English proverb

He is a man of sense who does not grieve for what he has not, but rejoices in what he has.

Epictetus

I believe that man will not merely endure, he will prevail. He is immortal not because he alone among creatures has an inexhaustible voice, but because he has a soul.

William Faulkner

You can easily judge the character of others by how they treat those who can do nothing for them or to them.

Malcolm Forbes

We are shaped and fashioned by what we love.
Johann Wolfgang von Goethe

What is moral is what you feel good after and what is immoral is what you feel bad after.

Ernest Hemingway

For afterwards a man finds pleasure in his pains, when he has suffered long and wandered long. So I will tell you what you ask and seek to know.

Homer
The Odyssey

An inexhaustible good nature is one of the most precious gifts of heaven, spreading itself like oil over the troubled sea of thought, and keeping the mind smooth and equable in the roughest weather.
Washington Irving

Our greatest happiness does not depend on the condition of life in which chance has placed us, but is always the result of a good conscience, good health, occupation, and freedom in all just pursuits.

Thomas Jefferson

Honesty is the first chapter in the book of wisdom.

Thomas Jefferson

An appealing personality is not something grafted on from without. It is not like a coat of paint applied to a building or cosmetics used on the face. It is expressed through the body, the mind, the heart and the spirit. Although some persons seem to have been born with an exceptionally appealing personality, no one has a monopoly on it.

Edith Johnson

Two things fill the mind with ever new and increasing wonder and awe: the starry heavens above me, and the moral law within me.

Immanuel Kant

Character cannot be developed in ease and quiet. Only through experience of trial and suffering can the soul be strengthened, ambition inspired, and success achieved.

Helen Keller

When I do good, I feel good. When I do bad, I feel bad.

Abraham Lincoln

In character, in manners, in style, in all things, the supreme excellence is simplicity.

Henry Wadsworth Longfellow

There is only one way to achieve happiness on this terrestrial ball, and that is to have either a clear conscience, or none at all.

Ogden Nash

The growth of wisdom may be gauged accurately by the decline of ill temper.

Friedrich Nietzsche

What does not kill me makes me stronger.

Friedrich Nietzsche

Character is much easier kept than recovered.

Thomas Paine

I care not what others think of what I do, but I care very much about what I think of what I do: That is character!

Theodore Roosevelt

No legacy is so rich as honesty.

William Shakespeare

Whatever you are by nature, keep to it; never desert your line of talent. Be what nature intended you for, and you will succeed.

Sydney Smith

A happy man or woman is a better thing to find than a five-pound note. He or she is a radiating focus of goodwill; and their entrance into a room is as though another candle had been lighted.

Robert Louis Stevenson

To love deeply in one direction makes us more loving in all others.

Anne-Sophie Swetchine

Joy is a net of love by which you can catch souls.

Mother Teresa

Goodness is the only investment which never fails.

Henry David Thoreau

Do not expect that you will make any lasting impression on the world through intellectual power without the use of an equal amount of conscience and heart.

William Jewett Tucker

It is curious that physical courage should be so common, and moral courage so rare.

Mark Twain

Character is power.

Booker T. Washington

Character and personal force are the only investments that are worth anything.

Walt Whitman

Morals and values aren't something you learn; they are something you "catch."

Unknown

Citizenship

Posterity! You will never know how much it cost the present generation to preserve your freedom. I hope you will make good use of it.

John Quincy Adams

One should guard against preaching to young people success in the customary form as the main aim in life. The most important motive for work in school and in life is pleasure in work, pleasure in its result, and the knowledge of the value of the result to the community.

Albert Einstein

Nationalism is an infantile sickness. It is the measles of the human race.

Albert Einstein

Perfect freedom is as necessary to the health and vigor of commerce as it is to the health and vigor of citizenship.

Patrick Henry

John Adams and Thomas Jefferson were political enemies, but they became fast friends. And when they passed away on the same day, the last words of one of them was, "The country is safe. Jefferson still lives." And the last words of the other was, "John Adams will see that things go forward."

Harry Truman

Climbing

In climbing, you're trying to find the path of least resistance within the obstacle.

Lynn Hill

When men climb on a great mountain together, the rope between them is more than a mere physical aid to the ascent; it is a symbol of the spirit of the enterprise. It is a symbol of men banded together in a common effort of will and strength against their only true enemies: inertia, cowardice, greed, ignorance, and all weaknesses of the spirit.

Charles Houston

The essence of climbing is not limited to those out there making a name for themselves.

Lois LaRock

The best climber in the world is the one who's having the most fun.

Alex Lowe

What we get from [climbing] is just sheer joy. And joy is after all, the end of life. We do not live to eat and make money. We eat and make money to be able to enjoy life. That is what life means and what life is for.

George Leigh Mallory

Climbing is a metaphor for life itself. There is the aspiration and the uncertainty, the journey and the risk, the success and its concomitant satisfaction. Life on the wall becomes a simplified model of life in the harried world, a model with equal anguish, but one whose challenges are carved into perfect definition. We win here and we know we can win elsewhere.

Don Mellor

I see the usefulness of climbing not in the further development of technique, rather in the development of the instinct and proficiency of man to extend himself.

Reinhold Messner

All my life, people have asked the question, directly or indirectly. "Why in the hell do you climb mountains?" I can't explain this to other people. I love the physical exertion. I love the wind. I love the storms. I love the fresh air. I love the companionship in the outdoors. I love the reality. I love the change. I love the rejuvenating spirit. I love to feel oneness with nature. I'm hungry; I enjoy eating. I get thirsty; I enjoy the clear water. I enjoy being warm at night when it's cold outside. All these things are extremely enjoyable because, gosh, you're really feeling them, you're living them, your senses are really feeling. I can't explain it.

Paul Petzoldt

The guides who taught me always said, "Climb above all with your head. Always measure what you want to do, against what you are capable of doing. Mountaineering is above all a matter of conscience."

Sometimes a climb is born of a dream, an excitement, a spontaneous desire, often unreasoning; a love name, a shape, a story, a memory and there we are, committed to a summit. But there must come a time of calculation; the precise relationship between the need envisaged and the resources of the climber must be assessed, and the final decision emerges from this assessment. The climber should always bear this formula in mind. It is displeasing in its harshness, but it is essential. It must decide for or against a project.

Keep alive the spirit of the pioneers, look always with the eyes of a child; for to see, it is not enough to open the eyes; first one must open one's heart.

Gaston Rebuffat
Between Heaven and Earth

Climbing needs no justification, no more than does watching a sunrise, or listening to a great symphony, or falling in love. . . . Rock and ice and wind and the great blue canopy of the sky are not all that he finds upon the mountain tops. He discovers things about his own body and mind he had almost forgotten. . . . He learns what his legs are for, what his lungs are for, what the wise men of the old meant by "refreshment of the spirit". . . . He finds the divine harmony and simplicity of the natural world, and himself alive in it, a part of it.

James Ramsey Ullman
High Conquest

Commitment

You must act as if it is impossible to fail.

Ashanti proverb

Never, never, never, never give up.

Winston Churchill

Wherever you go, go with all your heart.

Confucius

If thy heart fails thee, climb not at all.

Queen Elizabeth I

Don't be afraid to take a big step if one is indicated. You can't cross a chasm in two small jumps.

David Lloyd George

The ultimate measure of a man is not where he stands in moments of comfort and convenience, but where he stands at times of challenge and controversy.

Martin Luther King, Jr.

Half-heartedness never won a battle.

William McKinley

Until one is committed there is hesitancy, the chance to draw back, always ineffectiveness. Concerning all acts of initiative there is one elementary truth, the ignorance of which kills countless ideas and splendid plans: that the moment one definitely commits oneself, then providence moves too. All sorts of things occur to help one that would never otherwise have occurred. A whole stream of events issues from the decision, raising in one's favor all manner of unforeseen incidents and meetings and material assistance, which no man would have dreamt would have come his way.

W. H. Murray

Life always gets harder towards the summit—the cold increases, responsibility increases.

Friedrich Nietzsche

Technique and ability alone do not get you to the top—it is the willpower that is most important. This willpower you cannot buy with money or be given by others—it rises from your heart.

Junko Tabei, first woman on Everest

Declare your intention, then make it happen.

Unknown

> If you think you are beaten, you are.
> If you think you dare not, you don't.
> If you like to win but think you can't,
> It's almost a cinch you won't.
> If you think you'll lose, you're lost,
> For out in the world we find

Success begins with a fellow's will.
It's all a state of mind.
If you think you're outclassed, you are.
You've got to think high to rise.
You've got to be sure of yourself before
You can ever win a prize.
Life's battles don't always go
To the stronger or faster man.
But soon or later, the person who wins
Is the person who thinks they can.

Unknown

The biggest temptation is to settle for too little.

Unknown

Communication

Say what you mean, and mean what you say.

American proverb

It is not from ourselves that we will learn to be better than we are.

Wendell Berry

The people to fear are not those who disagree with you, but those who disagree with you and are too cowardly to tell you.

Napoleon Bonaparte

Charm is a way of getting the answer "Yes" without having asked any clear question.

Albert Camus

I criticize by creation, not by finding fault.

Cicero

When the creations of a genius collide with the mind of a layman and produce an empty sound, there is little doubt as to which is at fault.

Salvadore Dali

If the people around you are spiteful and callous and will not hear you, fall down before them and beg their forgiveness; for in truth you are to blame for their not wanting to hear you.

Fyodor Dostoyevsky

Criticism should not be querulous or wasting, all knife and root puller, but guiding, instructive, inspiring.

Ralph Waldo Emerson

There is nothing wrong with having nothing to say . . . unless you insist on saying it.

Ralph Waldo Emerson

Mastery of language affords remarkable power.

Frantz Fanon

If there is any great secret of success in life, it lies in the ability to put yourself in the other person's place and to see things from his point of view—as well as your own.

Henry Ford

Nothing is as burdensome as a secret.

French proverb

Silence makes no mistakes.

French proverb

You can preach a better sermon with your life than with your lips.

Oliver Goldsmith

I detest the man who hides one thing in the depths of his heart and speaks forth another.

Homer

Good communication is as stimulating as black coffee, and just as hard to sleep after.

Anne Morrow Lindbergh

It all starts with self-reflection. Then you can know and empathize more profoundly with someone else.

Shirley MacLaine

The great enemy of clear language is insincerity. When there is a gap between one's real and one's declared aims, one turns, as it were, instinctively to long words and exhausted idioms, like a cuttle fish squirting out ink.

George Orwell

The best leaders, almost without exception and at every level, are master users of stories and symbols.

Tom Peters

The heart has reasons of which the reason has no knowledge.

George Santayana

Always acknowledge a fault quite frankly. This will throw those in authority off their guard and give you an opportunity to commit more.

Mark Twain

The true test of being comfortable with someone else is the ability to share silence.

Frank Tyger

Whosoever does not know how to recognize the faults of great men is incapable of estimating their perfections.

Voltaire

A half truth is a whole lie.

Yiddish proverb

Silent company is often more healing than words of advice.

Unknown

Community

It takes a village to raise a child.

African proverb

It takes a child to raise a village.

Unknown

No man is an island entire of itself; every man is a piece of the continent, a part of the main. . . . Any man's death diminishes me because I am involved in Mankind; and therefore never send to know for whom the bell tolls; it tolls for thee.

John Donne

The only true solution of our political and social problems lies in cultivating everywhere the spirit of brotherhood, of fellow feeling and understanding between man and man, and the willingness to treat a man as a man.

Theodore Roosevelt

Competence

Achieving competence in any skill is a continuing process of education through guided study and individual experimentation. It requires commitment and practice.

We are what we repeatedly do. Excellence then, is not an act, but a habit.

Aristotle

The gem cannot be polished without friction, nor man perfected without trials.

Chinese proverb

Genius is one percent inspiration and ninety-nine percent perspiration.

Thomas Edison

The winds and waves are always on the side of the ablest navigators.

Edward Gibbon

Buy gear that is "good enough" but learn to use it really well. Owning a paint brush doesn't make you an artist.

John Gookin

You drink your sweat in this world.

Kenyan proverb

A good carpenter makes almost as many mistakes as a bad carpenter, but the good carpenter takes the time to fix them all.

Dave Slovisky

There's one thing I count on in the Iditarod: myself.

Frank Teasley

The road to success is always under construction.

Lily Tomlin

If you don't take care of yourself, the best equipment in the world can't prevent frostbite.

Jonathan Waterman

We always find plenty of time to do things the right way, on our second try.

Unknown

Conflict Resolution

Whether the stone bumps the jug or the jug bumps the stone, it is bad for the jug.

American folk saying

It is more difficult to organize peace than to win war; but the fruits of victory will be lost if the peace is not well-organized.

Aristotle

On the subject of singing, the frog school and the lark school disagree.

Chinese proverb

The great task of peace is to work morals into it. The only sort of peace that will be read is one in which everybody takes his share of responsibility. World organizations and conferences will be of no value unless there is improvement in the relation of men to men.

Frederick Eggleston

No problem can be solved from the same consciousness that created it.

Albert Einstein

Focus on future solutions rather than past problems.

Gary Faris

You cannot shake hands with a clenched fist.

Indira Gandhi

Now that you are an elder, drop your weapons and use your head and wisdom instead.

Masai ceremonial closing statement
for the rite of passage from adolescence
(Masai youth carry metal spears; elders carry wooden staffs)

Where there is much desire to learn, there of necessity will be much arguing, much writing, many opinions; for opinion is but knowledge in the making.

John Milton

Tell me what ticks you off, and I will tell you what makes you tick.

Lloyd John Ogilvie

How poor are they who have not patience! What wound did ever heal but by degrees?

William Shakespeare

A peace is of the nature of a conquest. For them both parties nobly are subdued, and neither party loses.

William Shakespeare

To fulfill the hopes of democracy in our American adventure we must attempt to understand one another better, must try to avoid all unnecessary clash of personalities, and develop calmly, before situations arise, suitable techniques for the handling of our differences. No opinion at variance with ours should ever be permitted to threaten our basic human relationship with anyone.

J. Richard Sneed

Learn the wisdom of compromise, for it is better to bend a little than to break.

Jane Wells

Though not always called upon to condemn ourselves, it is always safe to suspect ourselves.

Richard Whately

There is luxury in self-reproach. When we blame ourselves, we feel no one else has a right to blame us.

Oscar Wilde

Conservation

Wilderness is an anchor to windward. Knowing it is there, we can also know that we are still a rich nation, tending our resources as we should—not a people in despair searching every last nook and cranny of our land for a board of lumber, a barrel of oil, a blade of grass, or a tank of water.

Clinton P. Anderson

To preach conservation at such a time, when all our resources, national and otherwise are being sacrificed in unprecedented measure, might seem to some anomalous, even ironical. . . . But we firmly believe, and now are more acutely aware than ever, that conservation is basically related to the peace of the world and the future of the race.

John Detweiler
Breaking New Ground

In the end, we conserve only what we love. We will love only what we understand. We will understand only what we are taught.

Baba Dioum

The Arctic has a call that is compelling. The distant mountains [of the Brooks Range in Alaska] make one want to go on and on over the next ridge and over the one beyond. The call is that of a wilderness known only to a few. . . . This last American wilderness must remain sacrosanct.

William O. Douglas

This man, one of the chief architects of the atomic bomb, so the story runs, was out wandering in the woods one day with a friend when he came upon a small tortoise. Overcome with pleasurable excitement, he took up the tortoise and started home, thinking to surprise his children with it. After a few steps he paused and surveyed the tortoise doubtfully. "What's the matter?" asked his friend.

Without responding, the great scientist slowly retraced his steps as precisely as possible, and gently set the turtle down upon the exact spot from which he had taken him.

Then he turned solemnly to his friend. "It just struck me," he said, "that, perhaps for one man, I have tampered enough with the universe."

Loren Eiseley
The Firmament of Time

Having to squeeze the last drop of utility out of the land has the same desperate finality as having to chop up the furniture to keep warm.

Aldo Leopold

To save every cog and wheel is the first precaution of intelligent tinkering.

Aldo Leopold
Round River

The good news is that Americans will, in increasing numbers, begin to value and protect the vast American Landscape. The bad news is that they may love it to death.

Charles E. Little
The American Land

The preservation of a few samples of undeveloped territory is one of the most clamant issues before us today. Just a few more years of hesitation and the only trace of that wilderness which has exerted such a fundamental influence in molding American character will lie in the musty pages of pioneer books. . . . To avoid this catastrophe demands immediate action.

Bob Marshall

The only thing we know for sure about the future is that it will be radically different from the past. In the face of this enormous uncertainty, the least we can do for future generations is to pass on as many of the planet's resources as possible.

Norman Myers

The great question . . . is, shall we surrender to our surroundings, or shall we make our peace with nature and begin to make reparations for the damage we have done to our air, our land, our water? Restoring nature to its natural state is a cause beyond party and beyond factions. It has become a common cause of all the people of America.

Richard M. Nixon
State of the Union Address, January 22, 1970

The ages have been at work on it and man can only mar it.

Theodore Roosevelt

Something will have gone out of us as a people if we ever let the remaining wilderness be destroyed; if we permit the last virgin forests to be turned into comic books and plastic cigarette cases; if we drive the few remaining members of the wild species into zoos or to extinction; if we pollute the last clean air and dirty the last clean streams and push our paved roads through the last of the silence, so that never again will Americans be free in their own country from the noise, the exhausts, the stinks of human and automotive waste.

Wallace Stegner

The long fight to save wild beauty represents democracy at its best. It requires citizens to practice the hardest of virtues—self-restraint.

Edwin Way Teale
Circle of the Seasons

Plans to protect air and water, wilderness and wildlife are in fact plans to protect man.

Stewart Udall

Leave it as it is.

Unknown

Desert

And nowhere is water so beautiful as in the desert for nowhere else is it so scarce. By definition. Water, like a human being or a tree or a bird or a song gains value by rarity, singularity, isolation. In a human climate water is common. In the desert each drop is precious.

Edward Abbey
Desert Solitaire

The canyon country does not always inspire love. To many it appears barren, hostile, repellent—a fearsome, mostly waterless land of rock and heat, sand dunes and quicksand, cactus, thornbush, scorpion, rattlesnake, and agoraphobic distances. To those who see our land in that manner, the best reply is, yes, you are right, it is a dangerous and terrible place. Enter at your own risk. Carry water. Avoid the noonday sun. Try to ignore the vultures. Pray frequently.

Edward Abbey
The Journey Home

Diversity

Courtesy gives its owner a passport round the world. It transmutes aliens into trusting friends.

James Thomas Fields

I am both limited by my gender and empowered by it; I am both limited by my race and empowered by it. How do I name that, and at the same time understand that I'm more than that, and understand that I can be more than that with others? Understand that love can diminish the historical signification of oppression and exploitation? . . . Why is the fire of love not burning so hot that we have not even a moment to think about race, class or gender? This is a question that we have to ask ourselves as we light the fires of compassion within us, as we burn away our own fear.

bell hooks
The Heart of Learning

Tolerance is the positive and cordial effort to understand another's beliefs, practices and habits without necessarily sharing or accepting them.

Joshua Liebman

Endurance

It ain't over 'til it's over.

Yogi Berra

Press on: nothing can take the place of perseverance.
Talent will not; nothing is more common than
        unsuccessful men with talent.
Genius will not; unrewarded genius is almost a proverb.
Education will not; the world is full of educated
        derelicts.
Persistence and determination alone are omnipotent.
Press on!

Calvin Coolidge

Spend all day doing some marathon event, and you've finally invested the time and energy where you can *start* developing your endurance: this is the time to discipline yourself to stand proud, walk tall, and maintain a calm demeanor. You are conditioning yourself to maintain your energy through your posture, awareness and attitude. Collapse in a heap and you've wasted the perfect opportunity, unless of course you want to start all over the next day and work on self-improvement after running the same marathon again.

Jack Morman

Let us build up physical fitness for the sake of the soul.

Plato

We glory in the physical regeneration which is the product of our exertions; we exult over the grandeur of the scenes that are brought before our eyes, the splendors of sunrise and sunset, and the beauties of hill, dale, lake, wood, and waterfall; but we value more highly the development of manliness, and the evolution, under combat with difficulties, of those noble qualities of human nature: courage, patience, endurance, and fortitude.

Edward Whymper

Environmental Ethics

On a larger scale, a wildland ethic must be part of a more encompassing land or environmental ethic which is expressed every day.

Wendell Berry

The tree which moves some to tears of joy is in the eyes of others only a green thing that stands in the way.

William Blake

I am partial . . . to the moving trip that can give the visitor the feel of a big, continuous wilderness—one in which you can cross pass after pass, and know that on the other side you don't drop into civilization, but stay in wilderness instead. In big wilderness, you learn how important size itself is to the viability of the wilderness. It needs enough buffer to keep its heartland essentially free from the pervasive influences of technology. Such big wilderness is scarce, and is vanishing at a rate of about a million acres a year, chiefly to the chainsaw. People who know it can save it. No one else.

David Brower
Gentle Wilderness

Every American in every city in America will breathe clean air [early in the 21st century]. Ours is a rare opportunity to reverse the errors of this generation in service to the next. It's time to clear the air. . . . The wounded winds of north, south, east, and west can be purified and cleansed, and the integrity of nature can be made whole again.

George Herbert Walker Bush

A revolting state of affairs has elevated those non-producers advocating total harmony with our cosmic environment to near sainthood while concurrently condemning those of us responsible for utilizing the earth's resources in a futile effort to provide civil improvements.

Dave Canning

The "control of nature" is a phrase conceived in arrogance, born of the Neanderthal age of biology and philosophy when it was supposed that nature exists for the convenience of man.

Rachel Carson

The earth's vegetation is part of a web of life in which there are intimate and essential relations between plants and the earth, between plants and other plants, between plants and animals. Sometimes we have no choice but to disturb these relationships, but we should do so thoughtfully, with full awareness that what we do may have consequences remote in time and place.

Rachel Carson

The Four Laws of Ecology:
1. Everything is connected to everything else.
2. Everything must go somewhere.
3. Nature knows best.
4. There is no such thing as a free lunch.

Barry Commoner
The Closing Circle

All things in the biosphere have an equal right to live and to blossom and to reach their own individual forms of unfolding and self-realization.

Bill Devall and George Sessions
Deep Ecology

We believe the apocalypse is at hand, and the reasons for that belief are overwhelming: chemical and biological weapons, nuclear proliferation, deforestation, the greenhouse effect, ozone depletion, acid rain, the poisoning of our air and water, rising racism, massive species loss, toxic waste, the AIDS pandemic, the continuing population explosion, encroaching Big Brotherism, and at least a thousand points of blight. These aren't just conversation topics for yuppie cocktail parties; they're grade-A, unadulterated harbingers of destruction, 100 percent bona-fide specters of doom, and they're all proof that we don't need God to end it for us. The coming end will be strictly a do-it-yourself apocalypse.

Telephone hotline message from DOOM
(Society for Secular Armageddonism)

Love the animals, love the plants, love everything. If you love everything, you will perceive the divine mystery in things. Once you perceive it, you will begin to comprehend it better every day. And you will come at last to love the whole world with an all-embracing love.

Fyodor Dostoyevsky
The Brothers Karamazov

A human being is part of a whole, called by us the "Universe," a part limited in time and space. He experiences himself, his thoughts and feelings, as something separated from the rest—a kind of optical delusion of his consciousness. This delusion is a kind of prison for us, restricting us to our personal desires and to affection for a few persons nearest us. Our task must be to free ourselves from this prison by widening our circles of compassion to embrace all living creatures and the whole of nature in its beauty.

Albert Einstein

I have just about reached the conclusion that, while large industry is important, fresh air and clean water are more important, and the day may well come when we have to lay that kind of hand on the table and see who is bluffing.

Barry Goldwater

If we all treated others as we wished to be treated ourselves, then decency and stability would have to prevail. I suggest that we execute such a pact with our planet.

Stephen Jay Gould

What America does not do well is anticipate and avoid problems. Unfortunately, many environmental phenomena involve thresholds that, when passed, cause damage that is essentially irreversible. If we wait until the damage occurs and then respond, it will be too late.

Denis Hayes

If we are willing to risk military engagement to ensure the supply of Persian Gulf oil, does it make sense to propose cuts in energy conservation programs that will help reduce our dependence on that oil?

John Heinz
speech to the U.S. Senate, 1987

The supreme reality of our time is . . . the vulnerability of our planet.

John F. Kennedy

Examine each question in terms of what is ethically right, as well as what is economically expedient. A thing is right when it tends to preserve the integrity, stability, and beauty of the biotic community. It is wrong when it tends otherwise.

Aldo Leopold
A Sand County Almanac

A nation may be said to consist of its territory, its people, and its laws. The territory is the only part which is of certain durability. Laws change, people die, the land remains.

Abraham Lincoln

Our ideals, laws and customs should be based on the proposition that each, in turn, becomes the custodian rather than the absolute owner of our resources and each generation has the obligation to pass this inheritance on to the future.

Charles Lindbergh

In our way of life . . . with every decision we make, we always keep in mind the seventh generation of children to come. . . . When we walk upon Mother Earth, we always plant our feet carefully, because we know that the faces of future generations are looking up at us from beneath the ground. We never forget them.

Oren Lyons, Faithkeeper of the Onandaga Nation

Sooner or later in every talk, [David] Brower describes the creation of the world. He invites his listeners to consider the six days of Genesis as a figure of speech for what has in fact been 4 billion years. On this scale, one day equals something like six hundred and sixty-six million years, and thus, all day Monday and until Tuesday noon, creation was busy getting the world going. Life began Tuesday noon, and the beautiful organic wholeness of it developed over the next four days. At 4 p.m. Saturday, the big reptiles came on. At three minutes before midnight on the last day, man appeared. At one-fourth of a second before midnight Christ arrived. At one-fortieth of a second before midnight, the Industrial Revolution began. We are surrounded with people who think that what we have been doing for that one-fortieth of a second can go on indefinitely. They are considered normal, *but they are stark, raving mad.*

John McPhee
Encounters with the Archdruid

The Gaia Hypothesis asserts that Earth's atmosphere is continually interacting with geology (the lithosphere), Earth's cycling waters (the hydrosphere), and everything that lives (the biosphere). . . . The image is that the atmosphere is a circulatory system for life's biochemical interplay. If the atmosphere is part of a larger whole that has some of the qualities of an organism, one of those qualities we must now pray for is resilience.

Stephanie Mills
In Praise of Nature

Take nothing but pictures, kill nothing but time, leave nothing but footprints.

Motto, National Speleological Society

What a strange creature man is that he fouls his own nest.

Richard M. Nixon

We are the generation that searched on Mars for evidence of life, but couldn't rouse enough moral sense to stop the destruction of even the grandest manifestations of life on earth. In that sense, we are like the Romans whose works of art, architecture, and engineering inspire our awe but whose traffic in slaves and gladiatorial combat is mystifying and loathsome.

Roger Payne and Anna Sequoia
67 Ways to Save the Animals

We want them to use the education to be leaders in their community with an understanding of ecology and conservation for the wild outdoors far beyond their legislators back home. We expect these people to be a grain of sand on the beach of future leadership.

Paul Petzoldt

Conservation is the foresighted utilization, preservation, and/or renewal of forest, waters, lands and minerals, for the greatest good of the greatest number for the longest time.

Gifford Pinchot

We believe that interest in nature leads to knowledge,
which is followed by understanding,
and later, appreciation.
Once respect is gained
it is a short step to responsibility,

and ultimately action
to preserve our Earth.

Ian Player

The term ecology comes from the Greek word oikos, and means "the household." Ecological responsibility, then, begins at home and expands to fill the entire planet.

Jeremy Rifkin
The Green Lifestyle Handbook

At first, the people talking about ecology were only defending the fishes, the animals, the forest, and the river. They didn't realize that human beings were in the forest—and that these humans were the real ecologists, because they couldn't live without the forest and the forest couldn't be saved without them.

Osmarino Amancio Rodrigues
as quoted in The Burning Season by Andrew Revkin

The nation behaves well if it treats the natural resources as assets which it must turn over to the next generation increased and not impaired in value. Conservation means development as much as it does protection.

Theodore Roosevelt

The basis for any real morality must be the sense of kinship between all living things.

Henry Salt
The Creed of Kinship

Chief Seattle's Testimony

The Great Chief in Washington sends word that he wishes to buy our land. The Great Chief also sends words of his friendship and good will. This is kind of him, since we know he has little need of our friendship in return. But we will consider your offer. For we know that if we do not sell, the white man may come with guns and take our land.

How can you buy or sell the sky, the warmth of the land? The idea is strange to us. If we do not own the freshness of the air and the sparkle of the water, how can you buy them?

Every part of this earth is sacred to my people. Every shining pine needle, every sandy shore, every mist in the dark woods, every clearing, and humming insect is holy in the memory and experience of my people. The sap which courses through the trees carries the memories of the red man. The white man's dead forget the country of their birth when they go to walk among the stars. Our dead never forget this beautiful earth, for it is the mother of the red man. We are part of the earth and it is part of us. The perfumed flowers are our sisters; the deer, the horse, the great eagle, these are our brothers. The rocky crests, the juices of the meadows, the body heat of the pony, and man—all belong to the same family. So, when the Great Chief in Washington sends word that he wishes to buy our land, he asks much of us.

The Great Chief sends his word he will reserve us a place so that we can live comfortably to ourselves. He will be our father and we will be his children. So we will consider your offer to buy our land. But it will not be easy. For this land is sacred to us. The shining water that moves in the streams and rivers is not just water, but the blood of our ancestors. If we sell you land, you must remember that it is sacred, and you must teach your children that it is sacred and that each ghostly refection in the clear water of the lakes tells of events and memories in the life of my people.

The water's murmur is the voice of my father's father. The rivers are our brothers, they quench our thirst. The rivers carry our canoes and feed our children. If we sell you our lands, you must remember, and teach your children, that the rivers are our brothers, and yours. And you must henceforth give the rivers the kindness you would give any brother. The red man has always retreated before the advancing white man, as the mist of the mountains runs before the morning sun. But the ashes of our fathers are sacred. Their graves are holy ground, and so these hills, these trees, this portion of the earth is consecrated to us. We know that the white man does not understand our ways. One portion of land is the same to him as the next, for he is a stranger who comes in the night, and takes from the land whatever he

needs. The earth is not his brother, but his enemy, and when he has
conquered it, he moves on. He leaves his father's graves behind. His
father's graves and his children's birthright are forgotten. He treats
his mother, the earth, and his brother, the sky, as things to be bought
and leaves behind only a desert. I do not know why. Our ways are
different from your ways. The sight of your cities pains the eyes of
the red man. But perhaps it is because the red man is a savage and
does not understand.

There is no quiet place in the white man's cities. No place to hear
the unfurling of leaves in spring or the rustle of insect's wings. But
perhaps it is because I am a savage and do not understand. The clat-
ter only seems to insult the ears.

And what is there to life if a man cannot hear the lonely cry of the
whippoorwill or the arguments of the frogs around a pond at night? I
am a red man and do not understand.

The Indian prefers the soft sound of the wind darting over the face
of a pond, and the smell of the wind itself, cleansed by a midday rain
or scented with the pinion pine. The air is precious to the red man,
for all things share the same breath—the beasts, the tree, the man,
they all share the same breath. The white man does not seem to
notice the air he breathes. Like a man dying for many days, he is
numb to the stench.

But if we sell you our land, you must remember that the air is precious to us, that the air shares its spirit with the life it supports. The
wind that gave our grandfather his first breath also receives his last
sigh. And if we sell you our land, you must keep it apart and sacred,
as a place where even the white man can go to taste the wind that is
sweetened by the meadow's flowers.

So we will consider your offer to buy our land. If we decide to
accept, I will make one condition: the white man must treat the
beasts of this land as his brothers. I am a savage and do not understand any other way. I have seen a thousand rotting buffaloes on the
prairie, left by the white man who shot them from a passing train. I
am a savage and I do not understand how the smoking iron horse can
be more important than the buffalo that we kill only to stay alive.
What is man without the beasts? If all the beasts were gone, men
would die from a great loneliness of spirit. For whatever happens to

the beasts, soon happens to man. All things are connected. You must teach your children that the ground beneath their feet is the ashes of our grandfathers. So that they will respect the land, tell your children what we have taught our children, that the earth is our mother. Whatever befalls the earth befalls the sons of the earth. If men spit upon the ground, they spit upon themselves. This we know.

All things are connected like the blood which unites one family. All things are connected. Whatever befalls the earth, befalls the sons and daughters of the earth. Man did not weave the web of life, he is merely a strand in it. Whatever he does to the web, he does to himself. But we will consider your offer to go to the reservation you have for my people. We will live apart, and in peace. It matters little where we spend the rest of our days. Our children have seen their fathers humble in defeat. Our warriors have felt shame, and after defeat they turn their days in idleness and contaminate their bodies with sweet foods and strong drink. It matters little where we pass the rest of our days. They are not many. A few more hours, a few more winters, and none of the children of the great tribes that once lived on this earth or that roam it now in small bands in the woods will be left to mourn the graves of a people once as powerful and as hopeful as yours. But why should I mourn the passing of my people? Tribes are made of men, nothing more. Men come and go, like the waves of the sea. Even the white man, whose God walks and talks with him as friend to friend, shall see. One thing we know, which white men may one day discover—our God is the same God. You may think now that you own him as you wish to own our land, but you cannot.

Chief Seattle
speech at an 1854 tribal assembly
concerning the sale of land to the U.S. government

A fundamental difference appears between Schweitzer's principle of reverence for life, which proclaims the intrinsic and sacred value for life itself—"A man is ethical only when life, as such, is sacred to him"—and the seeming worship of the ecological niche, which is but a worship of our physical resources.

Henryk Skolimowski
Eco-Philosophy

We are the most dangerous species of life on the planet, and every other species, even the earth itself, has cause to fear our power to exterminate. But we are also the only species which, when it chooses to do so, will go to great effort to save what it might destroy.

Wallace Stegner

We travel together, passengers on a little space ship, dependent on its vulnerable reserves of air and soil, all committed for our safety to its security and peace, preserved from annihilation only by the care, the work, and, I will say, the love we give our fragile craft. We cannot maintain it half fortunate, half miserable, half confident, half despairing, half slave—to the ancient enemies of man—half free in a liberation of resources undreamed of until this day. No craft, no crew can travel safely with such vast contradictions. On their resolution depends the survival of us all.

Adlai Stevenson
speech to the UN, 1965

There was an eighty-seven year hiatus from the Declaration of Independence to the Emancipation Proclamation and the freeing of American Blacks from slavery. . . . The idea of an inalienable right of self-determination has moved with irresistible force to become what Jefferson claimed it was in 1776: a self-evident truth. . . . It is now nature's turn to be liberated.

Donald Worster and Roderick F. Nash
The Rights of Nature

Expedition Behavior

Equals make the best friends.

Aesop

What goes around, comes around.

American proverb

God is not kind to those who are not kind to others.

Arabian proverb

Do good. This should be the aim of every human being, to make the world better for having lived.

Eldress Harriet Bullard

The work an unknown good person has done is like a vein of water flowing hidden underground, secretly making the ground green.

Thomas Carlyle

Good manners are, to particular societies, what good morals are to society in general: their cement and their security.

Lord Chesterfield

We should render a service to a friend to bind them closer to us, and to an enemy to make a friend of him.

Cleobulus

He who confers a favor should at once forget it, if he is not to show a sordid, ungenerous spirit. To remind a man of kindness conferred upon him, and talk of it, is little different from reproach.

Demosthenes

It is one of the most beautiful compensations of this life that no man can help another without helping himself.

Ralph Waldo Emerson

A single sunbeam is enough to drive away many shadows.

St. Francis of Assisi

You reap what you sow.

Galatians 6:7

Ninety percent of the art of living consists of getting on with people one cannot stand.

Samuel Goldwyn

Your position never gives you the right to command. It only imposes on you the duty of living your life that others can receive your orders without being humiliated.

Dag Hammarskjold

Those who are at war with others are not at peace with themselves.

William Hazlitt

It is easier to love humanity as a whole than to love one's neighbor.

Eric Hoffer

Even after the heaviest storm the birds come out singing.

Rose Kennedy

We must learn to live together as brothers or perish together as fools.

Martin Luther King, Jr.

The way to do is to be.

Lao Tzu

Manners are a sensitive awareness of the feeling of others. If you have that awareness, you have good manners, no matter what fork you use.

Emily Post

The most important single ingredient in the formula of success is knowing how to get along with people.

Theodore Roosevelt

It is the weak who are cruel. Gentleness can only be expected from the strong.

Leo Rosten

He who allows his day to pass by without practicing generosity and enjoying life's pleasures is like a blacksmith's bellows—he breathes, but he does not live.

Sanskrit proverb

One thing I know: the only ones among you who will be really happy will be those who will have sought and found how to serve.

Albert Schweitzer

He that does good to another also does good to himself.

Seneca

Kind words can be short and easy to speak, but their echoes are truly endless.

Mother Teresa

Be gentle to all, and stern with yourself.

St. Teresa of Avila

Don't worry about returning favors: pass them on.

Pearl VanNatta

A sure way to lift oneself up is by helping to lift someone else.

Booker T. Washington

Favors cease to be favors when there are conditions attached to them.

Thornton Wilder

Expedition Planning

If you don't know where you're going, you'll end up somewhere else.

Yogi Berra

New boots . . . big steps.

Chinese proverb

It wasn't raining when Noah built the ark.

Richard Cushing

Nobody can really guarantee the future. The best we can do is size up the chances, calculate the risks involved, estimate our ability to deal with them and then make our plans with confidence.

Henry Ford II

There are two ways of being happy: We must either diminish our wants or augment our means.

Benjamin Franklin

By failing to prepare, you are preparing to fail.

Benjamin Franklin

If you don't know where you're going, every road will get you nowhere.

Henry Kissinger

Double-check your knot *before* you leave the ground.

Alison Osius

Never eat more than you can lift.

Miss Piggy

Beauty of style and harmony and grace and good rhythm depend on simplicity.

Plato

I think that we ought to eat all our Provisions now, so that we shan't have so much to carry.

Christopher Robin

Not all who wander are lost.

J. R. R. Tolkien

Brains first and then hard work.

Winnie the Pooh

Luck is a matter of preparation meeting opportunity.

Unknown

Experiential Education

Experiential education involves not just absorption of information, but also experience in real-life situations. Students take an active role in their education and apply what they have learned in the real world.

I find that a great part of the information I have was acquired by looking up something and finding something else on the way.

Franklin P. Adams

One must learn by doing the thing, for though you think you know it, you have no certainty until you try.

Aristotle

What we must learn to do, we learn by doing.

Aristotle

It takes most men five years to recover from a college education, and to learn that poetry is as vital to thinking as is knowledge.

Brooks Atkinson

Believe an expert: you will find something far greater in the woods than in books. Trees and stones will teach you that which you cannot learn from the masters.

St. Bernard of Clairvaux

Once the emotions have been aroused—a sense of the beautiful, the excitement of the new and unknown, a feeling of sympathy, pity, admiration or love—then we wish for the knowledge about the object of our emotional response. . . . It is more important to pave the way for the child to want to know than to put him on a steady diet of facts he is not ready to assimilate.

Rachel Carson

Give a man a fish and he eats for a day. Teach a man to fish and he eats for a lifetime.

Chinese proverb

To know that we know what we know, and that we do not know what we do not know, that is true knowledge.

Confucius

We live, and we learn, as much by unconscious absorption and imitation as by systematic effort.

Luella B. Cook

Experience does not err; only your judgments err by expecting from her what is not in her power.

Leonardo da Vinci

We may misunderstand, but we do not misexperience.

Vine Deloria, Jr.
Native American Testimony

A good education is usually harmful to a dancer. A good calf is better than a good head.

Agnes de Mille

We never understand a thing so well, and make it our own, as when we have discovered it for ourselves.

René Descartes

The human mind always makes progress, but it is a progress in spirals.

Madame de Staël

All genuine education comes through experience.

> John Dewey
> *Experience and Education*

Education is not preparation for life. Education is life.

> John Dewey

[Reflection enables] us to act in a deliberate and intentional fashion, . . . [to] convert action that is merely . . . blind and impulsive into intelligent action.

> John Dewey
> *How We Think: A Restatement of the Relation of*
> *Reflective Thinking to the Educative Process*

The intuitive mind is a sacred gift and the rational mind is a faithful servant. We have created a society that honors the servant and has forgotten the gift.

> Albert Einstein

The only source of knowledge is experience.

> Albert Einstein

For everything you have missed, you have gained something else.

> Ralph Waldo Emerson

Life is a series of experiences, each one of which makes us bigger, even though sometimes it is hard to realize this, for the world was built to develop character, and we must learn that the setbacks and griefs which we endure help us in our marching onward.

> Henry Ford

Do not try to satisfy your vanity by teaching a great many things. Awaken people's curiosity. It is enough to open minds; do not overload them. Put there just a spark. If there is some good inflammable stuff, it will catch fire.

> Anatole France

The ultimate goal of the educational system is to shift to the individual the burden of pursuing his own education.

John W. Gardner

It is the sin of the soul to force young people into opinions . . . but it is culpable neglect not to impel young people into experiences.

Kurt Hahn

There are three ways of trying to win the young. You can preach at them—that is a hook without a worm. You can say, "You must volunteer"—that is of the devil. And you can tell them, "You are needed"—that appeal hardly ever fails.

Kurt Hahn

> Give children the chance to discover themselves.
> See to it that children experience both success and defeat.
> See to it that there are periods of silence.
> Train the imagination, the ability to anticipate and to plan.
> Take sports and games seriously, but only as a part of the whole.
> Free the children of rich and influential parents from the paralyzing influence of wealth and privilege.
> Kurt Hahn's prescription for German education

The great value of formal education is that it is designed to foreshorten human experience. It endeavors with ease and economy to bring each succeeding generation up to date with respect to the past and to make it at home in the world. In this sense, it prepares each generation for life.

Virgil M. Hancher

I have but one lamp by which my feet are guided, and that is the lamp of experience.

Patrick Henry

Our world is a college, events are teachers, happiness is the graduating point, character is the diploma God gives man.

Hewell Dwight Hillis

In the deep, unwritten wisdom of life there are many things to be learned that can not be taught. We never know them by hearing them spoken, but we grow into them by experience and recognize them through understanding. Understanding is a great experience in itself, but it does not come through instruction.

Anthony Hope

Education's function is not to promote any propaganda, not to propound any principle as established and fixed for all time, not to assert that any belief is unchangeable, not to assert that any conclusion may not be mistaken—education's one and overwhelming responsibility is to establish the inquiring habit of mind and a veneration for truth.

Ernest Martin Hopkins

Experience is not what happens to you; it's what you do with what happens to you.

Aldous Huxley

Knowledge without wisdom is a bag of books on the back of an ass.

Japanese proverb

Understanding is more comprehensive than intellect because it invites truths that cautious intellect can get sight of but never embrace—like a sea-gazer who never plunges in. When we understand, we have left intellect on the shore and don't need it and its crabbed analyses.

David S. Jones

The best and most beautiful things in the world cannot be seen or even touched. They must be felt with the heart.

Helen Keller

Experience takes many of the things we already intuitively know, and gives us conviction.

Jim Lent

I try to leave students hungry at the end of class, never satiated.

Lucky Mallonee

If the only tool you have is a hammer, then you tend to see everything as a nail.

Abraham Maslow

If there is an art in teaching, it must be to make learning fun. In my classes I aim to give pleasure in the processes of learning, sharing with my students the pleasure I myself take in exploring the subject we are studying together.

Jeremy Murray-Brown

The surest way to corrupt a young man is to teach him to esteem more highly those who think alike than those who think differently.

Friedrich Nietzsche

There is a fine line between experiential education and instructor laziness.

Joe Nold

There are many arts among men, the knowledge of which is acquired bit by bit by experience. For it is experience that causes our life to move forward by the skill we acquire, while want of experience subjects us to the effects of chance.

Plato

Experience is the best teacher, but if you can get it second-hand the tuition is less.

Moisha Rosen

The great difficulty in education is to get experience out of ideas.

George Santayana

The vanity of teaching often tempteth a man to forget he is a block-head.

George Saville

Experience is a jewel, and it had need be so, for it is often purchased at an infinite rate.

William Shakespeare

Education is a private matter between the person and the world of knowledge and experience, and has little to do with school or college.

Lillian Smith

We should be careful to get out of an experience all the wisdom that is in it—not like the cat that sits down on a hot stove lid. She will never sit down on a hot stove lid again—and that is well; but also she will never sit down on a cold one anymore.

Mark Twain

There are two ways of spreading the light: to be the candle, or the mirror that reflects it.

Edith Wharton

Education is a journey, not a destination.

Unknown

Exploration, Adventure, and Discovery

The great obstacle to discovering the shape of the earth, the continents, and the ocean was not ignorance, but the illusion of knowledge.

Daniel J. Boorstin

Without a sense of the unknown and unknowable, life is flat and barren.

John Burroughs

To communicate wonder, we must have a spirit of wonder. A leader who's filled with wonder, joy and love for the natural world draws these good feelings out of others.

Joseph Cornell
Sharing the Joy of Nature

Adventure is worthwhile in itself.

Amelia Earhart

I am more of a sponge than an inventor. I absorb ideas from every source. I take half-matured schemes for mechanical development and make them practical. I am a sort of middleman between the long-haired and impractical inventor and the hard-headed businessman who measures all things in terms of dollars and cents. My principal business is giving commercial value to the brilliant but misdirected ideas of others.

Thomas Edison

The intellect has little to do on the road to discovery. There comes a leap in consciousness, call it intuition or what you will, and the solution comes to you and you don't know how or why. All great discoveries are made in this way.

Albert Einstein

The pursuit of truth and beauty is a sphere of activity in which we are permitted to remain children all our lives.

Albert Einstein

It's not that I'm so smart, it's just that I stay with problems longer.

Albert Einstein

If we knew what it was we were doing, it would not be called research, would it?

Albert Einstein

We have not ceased from exploration and the end of all our exploring will be to arrive where we started and know the place for the first time.

T. S. Eliot

For scientific discovery give me Scott; for speed and efficiency of travel, give me Admundson; but when disaster strikes and all hope is gone, get down on your knees and pray for Shackleton.

Edmund Hillary

Some set more by such things as come from a distance, but I recollect mother always used to maintain that folks was meant to be doctored with the stuff that grew right about 'em.

Sarah Orne Jewett

It's good to have an end to journey toward; but it is the journey that matters, in the end.

Ursula LeGuin

Satisfaction of one's curiosity is one of the greatest sources of happiness in life.

Linus Pauling

Adventure is not in the guidebook and beauty is not on the map. Seek and ye shall find.

Terry and Renny Russell

> The trails of the world be countless, and most of the
>   trails be tried;
> You tread on the heels of the many, 'til you come where
>   the ways divide;
> And one lies safe in the sunlight, and the other is dreary
>   and wan,
> Yet you look aslant at the Lone Trail, and the Lone Trail
>   lures you on.

Robert Service
from "The Lone Trail"

Put footsteps of courage into stirrups of patience.

Ernest Shackleton

Wisdom begins in wonder.

Socrates

> Afoot and lighthearted I take to the open roads
> Healthy and free, the world before me.
> The long brown path before me leading
> wherever I choose.
> Henceforth I ask not good fortune,
> I myself am good fortune.
> Henceforth I whimper no more,
> Postpone no more, need nothing,
> Done with indoor complaints, libraries,
> querulous criticisms.
> Strong and content I travel the open road.

Walt Whitman
from Leaves of Grass

It is travel into the unknown that frees the spirit and gives you a greater perspective on yourself.

Unknown

Failure and Success

Our greatest glory is not in never falling, but in rising every time we fall.

Confucius

Many of life's failures are people who did not realize how close they were to success when they gave up.

Thomas Edison

To laugh often and much;

To win the respect of intelligent people and the affection of children;

To earn the appreciation of honest critics and endure the betrayal of false friends;

To appreciate beauty, to find the best in others;

To leave the world a bit better, whether by a healthy child, a garden patch or a redeemed social condition;

To know even one life has breathed easier because you have lived.

This is to have succeeded.

Attributed to Ralph Waldo Emerson

Failure is success if we learn from it.

Malcolm Forbes

When I got cut from the varsity team as a sophomore in high school, I learned something. I knew I never wanted to feel that bad again. I never wanted to have that taste in my mouth, that hole in my stomach. So I set a goal of becoming a starter on the varsity.

Michael Jordan

Failure is, in a sense, the highway to success, inasmuch as every discovery of what is false leads us to seek earnestly after what is true.

John Keats

If at first you DO succeed, try something harder.

Ann Landers

When we can begin to take our failures non-seriously, it means we are ceasing to be afraid of them. It is of immense importance to learn to laugh at ourselves.

Katherine Mansfield

It's not the critic who counts, not the man who points out how the strong man stumbled or where the doer of deeds could have done them better. The credit belongs to the man who is actually in the arena; whose faith is marred by dust and sweat and blood; who errs and comes short again; who knows the great enthusiasms, the great devotions, and spends himself in a worthy cause; who, at the best, knows the triumph of high achievement; and who, at the worst, if he fails, at least fails while daring greatly, so that his place will never be with those cold and timid souls who know not victory nor defeat.

Theodore Roosevelt

Far better is it to dare mighty things, to win glorious triumphs, even though checkered with failure, than to rank with those poor spirits who neither enjoy much nor suffer much, because they live in the gray twilight that knows no victory or defeat.

Theodore Roosevelt

Fear and Courage

Action is the antidote to despair.

Joan Baez

It is to conquer fear that one becomes a climber. The climber experiences life to its extreme. A climber is not crazy. He is not out to get himself killed. He knows what life is worth. He is in love with living.

Walter Bonatti

Fool me once, shame on you. Fool me twice, shame on me.

Chinese proverb

Courage is what it takes to stand up and speak; courage is also what it takes to sit down and listen.

Winston Churchill

Nothing in life is to be feared. It is only to be understood.

Marie Curie

I'm afraid to be afraid.

> Catherine Destiville

A great part of courage is having done the thing before.

> Ralph Waldo Emerson

It is our attitude toward events, not events themselves, which we can control. Nothing is by its own nature calamitous—even death is terrible only if we fear it.

> Epictetus

A man who causes fear cannot be free from fear.

> Epicurus

There's nothing I'm afraid of like scared people.

> Robert Frost

He who is afraid of a thing gives it power over him.

> Moorish proverb

Courage is resistance to fear, mastery of fear—not absence of fear.

> Mark Twain

It is harder to kill a phantom than a reality.

> Virginia Woolf

Feedback

They that will not be counseled, cannot be helped.

> Benjamin Franklin

He who praises everybody praises nobody.

> Samuel Johnson

If it's very painful for you to criticize your friends—you're safe in doing it. But if you take the slightest pleasure in it, that's the time to hold your tongue.

Alice Duer Miller

Have you learned lessons only of those who admired you, and were tender with you, and stood aside for you? Have you not learned great lessons from those who rejected you, and braced themselves against you, or disputed the passage with you?

Walt Whitman

Fishing

I take fish personally, the way I take my life, like a sacrament. This is my body. Eat of it. Drink. I imagine this reverence is what they want of me.

Lorian Hemingway
The Gift of Trout

Fishing is a quest for knowledge and wonder as much as a pursuit of fish; it is as much an acquaintance with beavers, dippers, and other fishermen as it is the challenge of catching trout.

Paul Schullery
Mountain Time

If, as I suspect, trout fishing is something of a disease, then it is also something of a therapy in itself.

Tom Sutcliffe
Reflections on Fishing

The wildness and adventure that are in fishing still recommend it to me.

Henry David Thoreau
Walden

Fishermen are born honest, but they get over it.

Ed Zern
To Hell with Fishing

Friendship

No act of kindness, no matter how small, is ever wasted.

Aesop

The best compliment to a friend or child is the feeling you give them that they have been set free to make their own inquiries, to come to conclusions that are right for them, whether or not they coincide with your own.

Alistair Cooke

> May the road rise up to meet you,
> May the wind be always at your back.
> May the sun shine warm upon your face,
> And the rains fall soft upon your fields,
> And, until we meet again,
> May God hold you in the palm of His hand.
>
> Traditional Irish blessing

We are all travelers in the desert of life and the best we can find in our journey is an honest friend.

Robert Louis Stevenson

Friendship is the only cement that will hold the world together.

Woodrow Wilson

Hiking

Whenever possible I avoid the practice myself. If God had meant us to walk, he would have kept us down on all fours, with well-padded paws. He would have constructed our planet on the model of the simple cube, so that notion of circularity and consequently the wheel might never have arisen. He surely would not have made mountains.

There is something unnatural about walking. Especially walking uphill, which always seems to me not only unnatural but so unnecessary. That iron tug of gravitation should be all the reminder we need that in walking uphill we are violating a basic law of nature. Yet we persist in doing it. No one can explain why George H. Mallory's asinine rationale for climbing a mountain—"because it's there"—could easily be refuted with a few well-placed hydrogen bombs. But our common sense continues to lag far behind the available technology.

There are some good things to say about walking. Not many, but some. Walking takes longer, for example, than any other known form of locomotion except crawling. Thus, it stretches time and prolongs life. Life is already too short to waste on speed. I have a friend who's always in a hurry; he never gets anywhere. Walking makes the world much bigger and therefore more interesting. You have time to observe the details. The utopian technologists foresee a future for us in which distance is annihilated and anyone can transport himself anywhere, instantly. Big deal, Buckminster. To be everywhere at once is to be nowhere forever, if you ask me. That's God's job, not ours.

The longest journey begins with a single step, not with a turn of the ignition key. That's the best thing about walking, the journey itself. It doesn't matter whether you get where you're going or not. You get there anyway. Every good hike brings you eventually back home. Right where you started.

Which reminds me of circles. Which reminds me of wheels. Which reminds me my old truck needs another front-end job. Any good mechanics out there wandering along through the smog?

Edward Abbey

The thing to remember when traveling is that the trail is the thing, not the end of the trail. Travel too fast and you miss all that you are traveling for.

Louis L'Amour

Individuality

Constant togetherness is fine—but only for Siamese twins.

Victoria Billings

Many of our greatest American thinkers, men of the caliber of Thomas Jefferson, Henry Thoreau, Mark Twain, William James, and John Muir, have found the forest an effective stimulus to original thought.

Bob Marshall

To have one's individuality completely ignored is like being pushed quite out of life. Like being blown out as one blows out a light.

Evelyn Scott

The trouble with being in the rat race is that even if you win, you're still a rat.

Lily Tomlin

Initiative

A wise man will make more opportunities than he finds.

Francis Bacon

Making plans is always the fun part. Starting, doing and finishing are the hard parts.

Rollie Cox

Passion and vision are essential, but without *action* they are empty. It is easy to be immobilized by the sheer magnitude of the problems facing Earth, by tasks calling for Hercules when we know we are puny mortals. We feel daunted about demanding changes when we know that our lives are not pure, that we share the lifestyle that is ravaging the planet. We feel powerless in confronting the vast, immobile gray bureaucracy of government and industry.

"It's too much," we whimper, and surrender. "Better not to fight than to be defeated. Besides, where does one person start? I'm not an expert or a leader. Why don't *they* do something?"

We are frozen because the problems are too big. It's easier to turn on the TV, to plunge into the modern game (whoever dies with the most toys, wins!), to dull our expectations and passions with drink or with lines of white powder.

The Earth is crying. Do we hear? Martin Luther King, Jr., once said that if one has nothing worth dying for, one has nothing worth living for.

It is a time for courage.

There are many forms of courage. It takes courage to not allow your children to become addicted to television. It takes courage to tell the conservation group to which you belong, *No more compromise!* It takes courage to say no more growth in your community. It takes courage to say wild is more important than jobs. It takes courage to write letters to your local newspaper. It takes courage to stand up at a public hearing and speak. It takes courage to live a lower-impact life.

And it takes courage to put your body between the machine and the wilderness, to stand before the chain saw or the bulldozer.

In 1848, Henry David Thoreau went to jail for refusing, as a protest against the Mexican War, to pay his poll tax. When Ralph Waldo Emerson came to bail him out, Emerson said, "Henry, what are you doing in there?"

Thoreau quietly replied, "Ralph, what are you doing *out there*?"

Dave Foreman
Confessions of an Eco-Warrior

Nothing will ever be attempted if all possible objections must be first overcome.

Samuel Johnson

The journey of a thousand miles begins with one step.

Lao Tzu

In creating, the only hard thing is to begin.

James Russell Lowell

The beginning is the most important part of the work.

Plato

In mountaineering and exploration, efficiency does not depend on the amassing of material and manpower so much as the power to improvise plans at a moment's notice. In a word, to be adaptable. It is the opportunist who is most successful in the Himalayas.

Frank S. Smythe

She did observe, with some dismay, that, far from conquering all, love lazily sidestepped practical problems.

Jean Stafford

Go confidently in the direction of your dreams. Live the life you have imagined.

Henry David Thoreau

Everything I did in my life that was worthwhile I caught hell for.

Earl Warren

You always miss one hundred percent of the shots you don't take.

Unknown

Your world is as big as you make it.

Unknown

Judgment and Decision-Making

Better be wise by the misfortunes of others than by your own.

Aesop

Dear God, I pray for patience, and I want it right now!

Oren Arnold

There is no forgiveness in nature.

Ugo Betti

The only lasting trauma is the one we suffer without positive change.

Leo Buscaglia

Judgment is not on all occasions required, but prudence is.

Lord Chesterfield

Play for more than you can afford to lose, and you will learn the game.

Winston Churchill

A man who has committed a mistake and doesn't correct it is committing another mistake.

Confucius

There are two kinds of people who never amount to much—those who never do what they're told, and those who can do nothing else.

Cyrus H. K. Curtis

You need to understand the rules so you can break them intelligently.

The Dalai Lama

A handful of patience is better than a bushel of brains.

Dutch proverb

The important thing is to not stop questioning.

Albert Einstein

Nature always punishes any neglect of prudence.

Ralph Waldo Emerson

Common sense is genius dressed in its working clothes.

Ralph Waldo Emerson

On the occasion of every accident that befalls you, remember to turn to yourself and inquire what power you have for turning it to use.

Epictetus

The usual choice is not between the good and the bad, but between the bad and the worse.

French proverb

Basic research is what I am doing when I don't know what I am doing.

Thomas Fuller

Great ability without discretion comes almost invariably to a tragic end.

Leon-Michel Gambetta

An old error is always more popular than a new truth.

German proverb

The bravest person is the one who weighs up all the risks and when they have become greater than the object is worth, has the courage to turn back and to face the other risk of being called a coward.

Kurt Hahn

A warning is like an alarm clock: if you don't pay any heed to its ringing, some day it will go off and you won't hear it.

Sydney J. Harris

We fear things in proportion to our ignorance of them.

Livy

It is the momentary carelessness in easy places, the lapsed attention, or the wandering look that is the usual parent of disaster.

Albert F. Mummery

Whatever can go wrong, will.

Murphy's Law

The secret of knowing the fertile experiences and the greatest joys in life is to live dangerously.

Friedrich Nietzsche

There are old climbers and there are bold climbers, but there are no old, bold climbers.

Paul Petzoldt

Rules are for fools.

Paul Petzoldt

Sit down and have a cigarette after you do first aid, then plan your evacuation.

Paul Petzoldt

This is the real core of everything I have to teach, be it in the wilderness or in a book. Judgment. I define judgment as the ability to relate a total experience to a specific activity. Learning judgment, assessing priorities, is as important as perfecting techniques; in fact the teaching of techniques (without commensurate judgment) can be dangerous.

Paul Petzoldt
The Wilderness Handbook

It's criminal to teach a skill without teaching the adjoining judgment and ethics that go with it.

Paul Petzoldt

A man should never be ashamed to own that he has been in the wrong, which is but saying that he is wiser today than he was yesterday.

Alexander Pope

Trust also your own judgment, for it is your most reliable counselor. A man's mind has sometimes a way of telling him more than seven watchmen posted on a high tower.

Proverbs 26:16

Learn from the mistakes of others. You can't live long enough to make them all yourself.

Eleanor Roosevelt

Those who can't remember the past are doomed to repeat it.

George Santayana

The Inuit have no word for luck.

Paula Schiller

He may, with the good luck which sometimes attends children, drunkards, and persons with weak intellect, escape the dangers without even knowing that they were there. But if he affronts too often forces whose powers he had not attempted to understand, he will in the long run succumb.

Lord Schuster

To have a great adventure, and survive, requires good judgment. Good judgment comes from experience. Experience, of course, is the result of poor judgment.

Geoff Tabin

I mistrust the judgment of every man in a case in which his own wishes are concerned.

Duke of Wellington

Climb if you will, but remember that courage and strength are nothing without prudence, and that a momentary negligence may destroy the happiness of a lifetime.

Edward Whymper

Experience is simply the name we give our mistakes.

Oscar Wilde

If you don't learn from your mistakes, there's no sense making them.

Unknown

Leadership

The man whose authority is recent is always stern.

Aeschylus

Conductors of great symphony orchestras do not play every musical instrument; yet through leadership the ultimate production is an expressive and unified combination of tones.

Thomas D. Bailey

Power can be seen as power *with* rather than power *over*, and it can be used for competence and cooperation, rather than dominance and control.

Anne L. Barstow

A first-rate organizer is never in a hurry. She is never late. She always keeps up her sleeve a margin for the unexpected.

Arnold Bennett

A leader is a dealer in hope.

Napoleon Bonaparte

The price of greatness is responsibility.

Winston Churchill

Great spirits have always encountered violent opposition from mediocre minds.

Albert Einstein

A drop of honey catches more flies than a gallon of gall.

Folk saying

No one's a leader if there are no followers.

Malcolm Forbes

Laws too gentle are seldom obeyed; too severe, seldom executed.

Benjamin Franklin

Leaders have a significant role in creating the state of mind that is the society. They can serve as symbols of the moral unity of society. They can express the values that hold the society together. Most important, they can conceive and articulate goals that lift people out of their petty preoccupations, carry them above conflicts that tear a society apart, and unite them in the pursuit of objectives worthy of their best efforts.

John W. Gardner
No Easy Victories

What I do best is share my enthusiasm.

Bill Gates

Management is the capacity to handle multiple problems, neutralize various constituencies, motivate personnel. . . . Leadership, on the other hand, is an essentially moral act, not—as in most management—an essentially provocative act. It is the assertion of a vision, not simply an exercise of style.

A. Bartlett Giamatti

Those who can command themselves command others.

William Hazlitt

I make progress by having people around me who are smarter than I am—and listening to them. And I assume that everyone is smarter about something than I am.

Henry Kaiser

A leader is best when people barely know he exists, not so good when people obey and acclaim him, worse when they despise him. But of a good leader who talks little when his work is done and his aim fulfilled, they will say, "We did this ourselves."

Lao Tzu

He that is greatest among you shall be your servant.

Matthew 23:11

Confidence is contagious. So is lack of confidence.

Michael O'Brien

Never tell people how to do things. Tell them what to do and they will surprise you with their ingenuity.

George Patton

Leadership has to do with how people are. You don't teach people a different way of being, you create conditions so they can discover where their natural leadership comes from.

Peter Senge

Gentleness is a divine trait: nothing is so strong as gentleness, and nothing is so gentle as real strength.

Ralph W. Sockman

Greatness is a two-faced coin, and its reverse is humility.

Marguerite Stern

I am more afraid of an army of one hundred sheep led by a lion than an army of one hundred lions led by a sheep.

Charles-Maurice de Talleyrand-Périgord

Leading under fire is when the flame burns brightest, when we can
see what makes a difference. It is by examining these defining events
of the past, I believe, that we can best understand and remember
what we will need for our own leadership in the future.

Michael Useem
The Leadership Moment

We would rather have one man or woman working with us than three
merely working for us.

F. W. Woolworth

Leaders aren't born. They're made.

Unknown

Mountains

Men go back to the mountains, as they go back to sailing ships at
sea, because in the mountains and on the sea they must face up, as
did men of another age, to the challenge of nature. Modern man lives
in a highly synthetic kind of existence. He specializes in this and
that. Rarely does he test all his powers or find himself whole. But in
the hills and on the water the character of a man comes out.

Abram T. Collier

Climb the mountains and get their good tidings. Nature's peace will
flow into you as sunshine flows into trees. The winds will blow their
own freshness into you, and the storms their energy, while cares will
drop off like autumn leaves.

John Muir

Mountains should be climbed with as little effort as possible and
without desire. The reality of your own nature should determine
the speed. If you become restless, speed up. If you become winded,
slow down. You climb the mountain in an equilibrium between

restlessness and exhaustion. Then, when you're no longer thinking ahead, each footstep isn't just a means to an end but a unique event in itself. *This* leaf has jagged edges. *This* rock looks loose. From *this* place the snow is less visible, even though closer. These are things you should notice anyway. To live only for some future goal is shallow. It's the sides of the mountains which sustain life, not the top.

Robert Pirsig
Zen and the Art of Motorcycle Maintenance

Natural Rhythms

When we go down to the low-tide line, we enter a world that is as old as the Earth itself—the primeval meeting place of the elements of the Earth and water, a place of compromise and conflict and eternal change.

Rachel Carson

There is something infinitely healing in the repeated refrains of nature—the assurance that dawn comes after night, and spring after the winter.

Rachel Carson

Man is whole when he is in tune with the winds, the stars, and the hills. . . . Being in tune with the universe is the entire secret.

William O. Douglas

We should accept the cyclic pattern of Mother Nature's moods. The desert is not the enemy.

Farouk El-Baz

Adopt the pace of nature: her secret is patience.

Ralph Waldo Emerson

Nature knows no pause in progress and development, and attaches her curse on all inaction.

Johann Wolfgang von Goethe

All the sounds of the earth are like music.

Oscar Hammerstein

In nature there are neither rewards nor punishments; there are consequences.

Robert Ingersoll

Nature takes no account of even the most reasonable of human excuses.

Joseph Wood Krutch

We shall never achieve harmony with the land, any more than we shall achieve absolute justice or liberty for people. In these higher aspirations the important thing is not to achieve but to strive.

Aldo Leopold
A Sand County Almanac

Everybody needs beauty as well as bread, places to play in and pray in, where nature may heal and cheer and give strength to body and soul alike.

John Muir

In God's wildness lies the hope of the world—the great fresh, unlighted, unredeemed wilderness.

John Muir

Keep close to Nature's heart, yourself; and break clear away, once in a while, and climb a mountain or spend a week in the woods. Wash your spirit clean.

John Muir

The grand show is eternal. Eternal sunrise, eternal sunset, eternal dawn and gloaming, on seas and continents and islands, each in its turn, as the round earth rolls.

John Muir

Is not the sky a father and the earth a mother, and are not all living things with feet or wings or roots their children? Give me the strength to walk the soft earth, a relative to all that is!

John Neihardt
Black Elk Speaks

When man is happy, he is in harmony with himself and with his environment.

Oscar Wilde

The goal of life is living in agreement with nature.

Zeno

Observation

It's the frames which make some things important and some things forgotten. It's all only frames from which the content rises.

Eve Babitz

Rain! whose soft architectural hands have power to cut stones and chisel to shapes of grandeur the very mountains.

Henry Ward Beecher

The world can not be discovered by a journey of miles, no matter how long, but only by a spiritual journey, a journey of one inch, very arduous and humbling and joyful, by which we arrive at the ground at our feet, and learn to be at home.

Wendell Berry

The quality of life is in proportion, always, to the capacity for delight. The capacity for delight is the gift of paying attention.

Julia Cameron
The Artist's Way

I held a blue flower in my hand, probably a wild aster, wondering what its name was, and then thought that human names for natural things are superfluous. Nature herself does not name them. The important thing is to know this flower, look at its color until the blends become as real as a keynote of music. Look at the exquisite yellow flowerettes in the center, become very small with them. Be the flower, be the trees, the blowing grasses. Fly with the birds, jump with the squirrel!

Sally Carrighar
Home to the Wilderness

I like to think of nature as an unlimited broadcasting station, through which God speaks to us every hour, if we will only tune in.

George Washington Carver

You have to open yourself to natural spectacle, but willing it to happen is as difficult as willing yourself to fall in love. Like a child, you have to be empty of expectation, have to possess eyes that see and ears that hear. It takes practice, like anything.

Jerry Dennis
The River Home

Joy in looking and comprehending is nature's most beautiful gift.

Albert Einstein

The process of scientific discovery is, in effect, a continual flight from wonder.

Albert Einstein

I have come to see the nonsense of trying to describe fine scenery.

Nathaniel Hawthorne

Of what avail is an open eye, if the heart is blind?

Solomon Ibn-Gabirol

Long before I ever saw the desert I was aware of the mystical overtones which the observation of nature made audible to me. But I have never been more frequently or more vividly aware of them than in connection with the desert phenomena.

Joseph Wood Krutch
The Forgotten Peninsula

The real voyage of discovery consists not in seeking new landscapes but in having new eyes.

Marcel Proust

We simply need that wild country available to us, even if we never do more than drive to its edge and look in. For it can be a means of reassuring ourselves of our sanity as creatures, a part of the geography of hope.

Wallace Stegner

To Touch and Feel is to experience. Many people live out their entire lives without really Touching or being Touched by anything. These people live within a world of mind and imagination that may move them sometimes to joy, tears, happiness or sorrow. But these people never really Touch. They do not live and become one with life.

Hyemeyohsts Storm
Seven Arrows

No video, no photographs, no verbal descriptions, no lectures can provide the enchantment that a few minutes out-of-doors can: watch a spider construct a web; observe a caterpillar systematically ravaging the edge of a leaf; close your eyes, cup your hands behind your ears, and listen to aspen leaves rustle or a stream muse about its pools and eddies. Nothing can replace plucking a cluster of pine needles and rolling them in your fingers to feel how they're put together, or discovering that "sedges have edges and grasses are round." The

firsthand, right-and-left-brain experience of being in the out-of-doors
involves all the senses including some we've forgotten about, like
smelling water a mile away. No teacher, no student, can help but
sense and absorb the larger ecological rhythms at work here, and the
intertwining of intricate, varied and complex strands that characterize
a rich, healthy natural world.

Ann Zwinger
Into the Field: A Guide to Locally Focused Teaching

Oceans

I am not afraid of storms for I am learning how to sail my ship.

Louisa May Alcott

The edge of the sea is a strange and beautiful place. All through the
long history of Earth it has been an area of unrest where waves have
broken heavily against the land, where the tides have pressed forward
over the continents, receded, and then returned. For no two suc-
cessive days is the shore line precisely the same. Not only do the
tides advance and retreat in their eternal rhythms, but the level of the
sea itself is never at rest. It rises or falls as the glaciers melt or grow,
as the floor of the deep ocean basins shifts under its increasing load
of sediments, or as the Earth's crust along the continental margins
warps up or down in adjustment to strain and tension. Today a little
more land may belong to the sea, tomorrow a little less. Always the
edge of the sea remains an elusive and indefinable boundary.

Rachel Carson
The Edge of the Sea

The oceans are the planet's last great living wilderness, man's only
remaining frontier on Earth, and perhaps his last chance to prove
himself as a rational species.

John L. Culliney
The Forests of the Sea

Methods of fishing are becoming more and more efficient, but the whole fishing industry is based on the exploitation of a wild population. This is almost a prehistoric concept on land, but it has never been questioned at sea.

Duke of Edinburgh
Men, Machines, and Sacred Cows

A smooth sea never made a skilled mariner.

English proverb

If you wish to learn to pray, put to sea.

Portuguese proverb

A ship in a harbor is safe, but that is not what a ship is built for.

William Shedd

The great sea has sent me adrift.
It moves me as the weed in a great river.
Earth and the great weather move me, have carried me
away, and moved my inward parts with joy.

Uvavnuk, Inuit shaman

I cannot separate land and sea: to me they interfinger like a pattern in a moss agate, positive and negative shapes irrevocably interlocked. My knowledge of this peninsula depends on that understanding: of underwater canyons that are continuations of the land, of the shell fossils far inland that measure continuations of the sea in eons past.

Ann Zwinger

Paddling

To stick your hands into the river is to feel the cords that bind the earth together in one piece.

Barry Lopez

There is magic in the feel of a paddle and the movement of a canoe, a magic compounded of distance, adventure, solitude and peace. The way of a canoe is the way of the wilderness and of a freedom almost forgotten. It is an antidote to insecurity, the open door to waterways of ages past and a way of life with profound and abiding satisfactions.

Sigurd Olson

Recognize, don't memorize. You don't really become a good boat handler until you can feel what's around the corner. The river tells you what it's doing and what it's about to do.

Kenny Ross

Peak Performance

Courage and perseverance have a magical talisman, before which difficulties disappear and obstacles vanish into air.

John Quincy Adams

God is with those who patiently persevere.

Arabian proverb

Excellence is an art won by training and habituation. We do not act rightly because we have virtue or excellence, but we rather have those because we have acted rightly. We are what we repeatedly do. Excellence, then, is not an act but a habit.

Aristotle

Striving for excellence motivates you; striving for perfection is demoralizing.

Harriet Braiker

One cannot manage too many affairs. Like pumpkins in the water, one pops up while you try to hold down the other.

Chinese proverb

High, but not the highest intelligence, combined with the greatest degree of persistence, will achieve greater eminence than the highest degree of intelligence with somewhat less persistence.

Catherine M. Cox

Mediocrity finds safety in standardization.

Frederick E. Crane

In the realm of ideas, everything depends on enthusiasm; in the real world, all rests on perseverance.

Johann Wolfgang von Goethe

One can never consent to creep when one feels an impulse to soar.

Helen Keller

To play great music, you must keep your eyes on a distant star.

Yehudi Menuhin

I never use a score when conducting my orchestra. Does a lion tamer enter the cage with a book on how to tame a lion?

Dimitri Mitropolous

The race will go to the curious, the slightly mad and those with an unsated passion for learning and daredeviltry.

Tom Peters

I use not only all the brains I have but all I can borrow.

Woodrow Wilson

Positive Attitude

The trick is what one emphasizes. We either make ourselves miserable or we make ourselves strong. The amount of work is the same.

Carlos Castaneda

A pessimist sees the difficulty in every opportunity; an optimist sees the opportunity in every difficulty.

Winston Churchill

Choose a job you love, and you will never work a day in your life.

Confucius

Desiderata

Go placidly amid the noise and haste, and remember what peace there may be in silence.

As far as possible without surrender be on good terms with all persons. Speak your truth quietly and clearly; and listen to others, even the dull and ignorant; they too have their story.

Avoid loud and aggressive persons; they are vexations to the spirit. If you compare yourself with others, you may become vain and bitter, for always there will be greater and lesser persons than yourself. Enjoy your achievements as well as your plans.

Keep interested in your career, however humble; it is a real possession in the changing fortunes of time. Exercise caution in your business affairs, for the world is full of trickery. But let this not blind you to what virtue there is; many persons strive for high ideals; and everywhere life is full of heroism.

Be yourself. Especially do not feign affection. Neither be cynical about love; for in the face of all aridity and disenchantment it is as perennial as the grass.

Take kindly the counsel of the years, gracefully surrendering the things of youth. Nurture strength of spirit to shield you in sudden misfortune. But do not distress yourself with dark imaginings. Many fears are born of fatigue and loneliness. Beyond a wholesome discipline, be gentle with yourself.

You are a child of the universe, no less than the trees and the stars; you have a right to be here. And whether or not it is clear to you, no doubt the universe is unfolding as it should.

Therefore be at peace with God, whatever you conceive Him to be, and whatever your labors and aspirations, in the noisy confusion of life keep peace with your soul.

With all its sham, drudgery and broken dreams, it is still a beautiful world.

Be cheerful.

Strive to be happy.

Max Ehrmann

Happiness is not in strength, or wealth, or power, or in all three. It lives in ourselves.

Epictetus

There is a soul force in the universe which, if we permit it, will flow through us and produce miraculous results.

Mahatma Gandhi

Don't compromise yourself. You are all you've got.

Janis Joplin

Seize the day.

Latin proverb

We can complain because rose bushes have thorns, or we can rejoice that thorn bushes have roses.

Abraham Lincoln

Our deepest fear is not that we are inadequate. Our deepest fear is that we are powerful beyond measure. It is our light, not our darkness, that most frightens us. We ask ourselves, who am I to be brilliant, gorgeous, talented, fabulous? Actually, who are you not to be? You are a child of God; your playing small doesn't serve the world. There is nothing enlightened about shrinking so that other people won't feel insecure around you. We were born to make manifest the glory of God that is within us. It's not just in some of us; it's in everyone. And as we let our own light shine, we unconsciously give other people permission to do the same. As we are liberated from our own fear, our presence automatically liberates others.

Nelson Mandela
1994 inaugural speech

Those who don't know how to weep with their whole heart don't know how to laugh either.

Golda Meir

Some people walk in the rain; others just get wet.

Roger Miller

A bunch of Yukon gold miners had an arrangement where whoever complained about the cooking became the next cook. The first night of the new deal, someone complained that the moose steak was burned, so they became the cook, meaning they had to get up at 5 A.M., have breakfast ready by 7, had to leave the mine early to get dinner ready, stay up late and do the dishes, etc. etc. etc. It was a dreaded job for a miner. A week later, someone muttered that the coffee wasn't quite warm enough, so they inherited the job. The whole gang was pretty savvy now, so the same guy was stuck in the kitchen for over a month. He started getting worse and worse about the meal preparation, but everyone just choked down the burnt toast and spiceless meals. So one Sunday he left the mine extra early, telling everyone it was his mother's birthday and he wanted to make a special meal. He broiled the marinated moose roast to perfection. He made croissants. He cooked cranberries, mashed potatoes, and made the best meal he could imagine. And for dessert, he made a scrumptious pie crust, rolling it out extra thick. But he filled the crust with a jellied stew of fresh moose turds. He put on his cleanest clothes to serve the meal, and the miners were in absolute heaven as he brought out one dish after another. The whole time he kept telling them to save room for dessert, which would be the first dessert they'd had in two months. Finally, he brought the pie out and its golden crust was magnificent. It gently steamed into the room and the crust smelled heavenly. While it was sitting there he broke out a bottle of whiskey which he passed around in honor of his mother's birthday. Finally, he cut the pie. The first guy to taste it got a horrible look on his face, turned to the cook and said "This tastes like moose s——! But it sure is *good!*"

As told by Jack Niggemyer

No one can make you feel inferior without your consent.

Eleanor Roosevelt

Be a friend to yourself, and others will.

Scottish proverb

There is nothing either good or bad, but thinking makes it so.

William Shakespeare

> Look to this day,
> For it is life, the very life of life.
> In its brief course lie all the
> verities and realities of your existence:
> the bliss of growth, the glory of action,
> the splendor of beauty.
>
> For yesterday is but a dream and
> tomorrow is only a vision,
> but today well lived makes
> every yesterday a dream of happiness
> and every tomorrow a vision of hope.
>
> Look well, therefore, to this day.
> Such is the salutation of the dawn.

The Sufi

If you keep open your eyes of wisdom and calmness, you will see there is a lot of enjoyment in this world—just as though you are watching a motion picture.

Paramahansa Yogananda

A Zen Buddhist monk was climbing an overhanging cliff free solo. He couldn't get up the last move cleanly, so he grabbed a vegetation hold and carefully put some of his weight on it. The little bush pulled out and he noticed one fat ripe blueberry on it. He slowly lost his grip on the rock and fell into free space, still holding the blueberry bush.

Q: What did he do?

A: He ate the blueberry.

Unknown

Respect

Respect is appreciation of the *separateness* of the other person, of the ways in which he or she is unique.

Annie Gottlieb

When you are content to be simply yourself and don't compare or compete, everybody will respect you.

Lao Tzu

When we see land as a community to which we belong, we may begin to use it with love and respect.

Aldo Leopold
A Sand County Almanac

Self-respect is at the bottom of all good manners. They are the expression of discipline, of goodwill, of respect for other people's rights and comfort and feelings.

Edgar S. Martin

Wilderness itself is the basis of all our civilization. I wonder if we have enough reverence for life to concede to wilderness the right to live on?

Margaret Murie

If we were all expected to play the first violin, there would never be an ensemble. Therefore, respect every musician in his proper place.

Robert Schumann

We can not return to Eden. We know too much and we care too little about the complexities of our collective past. But perhaps we can find our way toward a new genesis, a wiser relationship toward Creation that is founded on the sacred principles of love and respect and empathy.

Terry Tempest Williams

To honor and respect means to think of the land and the water and plants and animals who live here as having a right equal to our own to be here. We are not the supreme and all-knowing beings, living at the top of the pinnacle of evolution, but in fact we are members of the sacred hoop of life, along with the trees and rocks, the coyotes and the eagles and fish and toads, that each fulfills its purpose. They each perform their given task in the sacred hoop, and we have one, too.

Wolf Song of the Abenaki tribe

Responsibility

Show me a person who can not bother to do little things, and I'll show you a person who can not be trusted to do big things.

Lawrence D. Bell

The ultimate test of a moral society is the kind of world that it leaves to its children.

Dietrich Bonhoeffer

Today always comes before tomorrow.

Botswani proverb

Dig a well before you are thirsty.

Chinese proverb

Do you think my climb will be counted as the first Italian success?
Claudio Corti, after his partner died and rescuers
hauled him up the North Face of The Eiger

Misfortunes always come in the door that has been left open for them.

> Czech proverb

Intelligence becomes ours in the degree in which we use it and accept responsibility for consequences.

> John Dewey
> *Human Nature and Conduct*

If you can't save your buddy, it's not the buddy system.

> Joel Dovenbarger, scuba instructor

No man is free who is not master of himself.

> Epictetus

He that riseth late must trot all day.

> Benjamin Franklin
> *Poor Richard's Almanac*

If you sleep 'til noon, you have no right to complain that the days are short.

> Thomas Fuller

If everyone sweeps before his own front door, then the street is clean.

> Johann Wolfgang von Goethe

There are little things you need to do on expeditions, to prepare for occasional glitches, like making sure your group has a first aid kit, sewing a torn sleeve, and maintaining your stove. Not doing any one of them is not usually a short-term problem. The main problem is your general lack of respect for potential problems, and that will eventually cost you dearly.

> John Gookin

We do not inherit the earth from our ancestors. We borrow it from our children.

> Haida Indian proverb

Freedom of speech does not give a person the right to shout "Fire" in a crowded theater.

Oliver Wendell Holmes

Injustice anywhere is a threat to justice everywhere.

Martin Luther King, Jr.

You can delegate authority, but you can never delegate the responsibility for delegating a task to someone else. If you picked the right person, fine, but if you picked the wrong person, the responsibility is yours—not theirs.

Richard E. Krafve

God gives talent; work transforms talent into genius.

Anna Pavlova

Commitment is not fashionable: cool is the order of the day. . . .
We face the possible loss of our most precious asset, Western democracy. . . . All because we are lazy, cynical and self-indulgent, unwilling to make the effort.

Felix Rohatyn

Work consists of whatever a body is obliged to do, and play consists of whatever a body is not obliged to do.

Mark Twain

The girl who can't dance says the band can't play.

Yiddish proverb

If you don't stand for something, you'll fall for anything.

Unknown

Rivers

If there is magic on this planet, it is contained in water.

Loren Eiseley

Eventually, all things merge into one, and a river runs through it. The river was cut by the world's great flood and runs over rocks from the basement of time. On some of the rocks are timeless raindrops. Under the rocks are the words, and some of the words are theirs. I am haunted by waters.

Norman Maclean
A River Runs Through It

Swift or smooth, broad as the Hudson or narrow enough to scrape your gunwales, every river is a world of its own, unique in pattern and personality. Each mile on a river will take you further from home than a hundred miles on a road.

Bob Marshall

As long as there are young people with the light of adventure in their eyes or a touch of wildness in their souls, rapids will be run.

Sigurd Olson

The whole state [California] thrives, even survives, by moving water from where it is, and presumably isn't needed, to where it isn't, and presumably is needed. No other state has done as much to fructify its deserts, make over its flora and fauna, and rearrange the hydrology God gave it. No other place has put as many people where they probably have no business being.

Marc Reisner
Cadillac Desert

There's no music like a little river's. . . . It takes the mind out of doors. . . . It quiets a man down like saying his prayers.

Robert Louis Stevenson
Prince Otto

It was kind of solemn, drifting down the big, still river, laying on our backs, looking up at stars, and we didn't even feel like talking aloud.

Mark Twain
The Adventures of Huckleberry Finn

For what is the West, what makes it distinctive, if not the infrequent, lifegiving rivers that wind and churn across the dry landscape, the open space, some of it kept truly wild, that lifts our vision and our minds?

Todd Wilkinson
The Eagle Bird: Mapping a New West

Self-Awareness

The chief executive who knows his strengths and weaknesses as a leader is likely to be far more effective than the one who remains blind to them. He also is on the road to humility, that priceless attitude of openness to life that can help a manager absorb mistakes, failures or personal shortcomings.

John Adair

It is not the eye that understands, but the mind.

African proverb

I count him braver who overcomes his desires than him who conquers his enemies, for the hardest victory is the victory over self.

Aristotle

Argue for your limitations and they are yours!

Richard Bach

You grow up the first day you have your first real laugh—at yourself.

Ethel Barrymore

He that fancies himself very enlightened, because he sees the deficiencies of others, may be very ignorant, because he has not studied his own.

Edward Bulwer-Lytton

We are so ruled by what people tell us we must be that we have forgotten who we are.

Leo Buscaglia

Every man is the painter and the sculptor of his own life.

St. John Chrysostom

We do not believe in ourselves until someone reveals that deep inside us something is valuable, worth listening to, worthy of our trust, sacred to our touch. Once we believe in ourselves we can risk curiosity, wonder, spontaneous delight or any experience that reveals the human spirit.

e. e. cummings

Do not wish to be anything but what you are, and to be that perfectly.

St. Francis de Sales

> You cannot stay on the summit forever,
> You have to come down again. . . .
> So why bother in the first place?
> Just this: what is above knows what is below
> But what is below does not know what is above.
> One climbs, one sees. One descends, one sees no longer.
> But one has seen.
> There is an art of conducting oneself in the lower
>   regions by the memory of what one saw higher up.

Rene Dumal

> It is easy in the world to live after the world's opinions;
> it is easy in solitude to live after your own;

but the great man is he who in the midst of the crowd
keeps with perfect sweetness the independence of
solitude.

Ralph Waldo Emerson

You come to understand yourself through understanding others. History is full of examples of philosophers and holy men who retired into the wilderness to ponder the mystery of self. But you can't learn to understand yourself by withdrawing to your mountain top or A-bomb shelter. The self, by which we mean the personality, exists chiefly in the appreciation and esteem of your fellows.

Richard Lake

Knowing others is wisdom. Knowing yourself is Enlightenment.

Lao Tzu

I hoped that the trip would be the best of all journeys: a journey into ourselves.

Shirley MacLaine

In order to see much one must learn to look away from oneself—every mountain climber needs this hardness. You must climb above yourself—up and beyond—until you have even your stars under you! Yes! To look down upon myself and even upon my stars: that alone would I call my summit, that has remained for me my ultimate summit.

Friedrich Nietzsche

The best way to stop a bad habit is to never begin it.

James C. Penney

Live each day as you would climb a mountain. An occasional glance towards the summit puts the goal in mind. Many beautiful scenes can be observed from each new vantage point. Climb steadily, slowly, enjoy each passing moment; and the view from the summit will serve as a fitting climax to the journey.

Joe Porcino

The unexamined life is not worth living.

Socrates

You cannot run away from a weakness. You must sometimes fight it out or perish; and if that be so, why not now, and where you stand?

Robert Louis Stevenson

Not till we are lost . . . do we begin to find ourselves.

Henry David Thoreau

It is better to ask some of the questions than to know all of the answers.

James Thurber

You get what you expect.

Unknown

Self-Differentiation

A self-differentiated person calls their own shots. They make choices based on a personal, well-developed sense of ethics rather than submitting to the opinions and desires of other people.

Love yourself first and everything else falls into line. You really have to love yourself to get anything done in this world.

Lucille Ball

The healthy and strong individual is the one who asks for help when he needs it, whether he's got an abscess on his knee or in his soul.

Rona Barrett

As time passes we all get better at blazing a trail through the thicket of advice.

Margot Bennett

That you may retain your self-respect: it is better to displease the people by doing what you know is right, than to temporarily please them by doing what you know is wrong.

William J. H. Boetcker

Self-reliance and self-respect are about as valuable commodities as we can carry in our pack through life.

Luther Burbank

Be not disturbed at being misunderstood. Be disturbed rather at not being understanding.

Chinese proverb

An insult is either sustained or destroyed, not by the disposition of those who insult, but by the disposition of those who bear it.

St. John Chrysostom

The wise men of antiquity, when they wished to make the whole world peaceful and happy, first put their own states into proper order.

Confucius

He who permits himself to be insulted deserves the insult.

Pierre Corneille

I don't know the formula for success. But I do know that the formula that guarantees failure is trying to please everybody.

Bill Cosby

Small is the number of them that see with their own eyes and feel with their own hearts.

Albert Einstein

In order to be an immaculate member of a flock of sheep, one must above all be a sheep oneself.

Albert Einstein

Desire for approval and recognition is a healthy motive, but the desire to be acknowledged as better, stronger or more intelligent than a fellow being or fellow scholar easily leads to an excessively egoistic psychological adjustment, which may become injurious for the individual and for the community.

Albert Einstein

Nothing can bring you peace but yourself. Nothing can bring you peace but the triumph of principles.

Ralph Waldo Emerson
Self-Reliance

I was raised to sense what someone wanted me to be and be that kind of person. It took me a long time not to judge myself through someone else's eyes.

Sally Field

The eyes of other people are the eyes that ruin us.

Benjamin Franklin

As soon as you trust yourself, you will know how to live.

Johann Wolfgang von Goethe

Secure your standing place and you can move the world.

Johann Wolfgang von Goethe

Everybody wants to be somebody, but nobody wants to grow.

Johann Wolfgang von Goethe

When we describe what the other person is really like, I suppose we often picture what we want. We look through the prism of our need.

Ellen Goodman

My mother drew a distinction between achievement and success. She said that achievement is the knowledge that you have studied and worked hard and done the best that is in you. Success is being praised by others, and that's nice, too, but not as important or satisfying. Always aim for achievement and forget about success.

Helen Hayes

We are taught you must blame your father, your sisters, your brothers, the school, the teachers—you can blame anyone, but never blame yourself. It's never your fault. But it's always your fault, because if you wanted to change, you're the one who has to change. It's as simple as that, isn't it?

Katharine Hepburn

He who conquers others is strong. He who conquers himself is mighty.

Lao Tzu

Think wrongly, if you please, but in all cases think for yourself.

Doris Lessing

He that respects himself is safe from others; he wears a coat of mail that none can pierce.

Henry Wadsworth Longfellow

Don't be so humble—you're not that great.

Golda Meir

I didn't belong as a kid, and that always bothered me. If only I'd known that one day my differentness would be an asset, then my early life would have been much easier.

Bette Midler

Self-government, self-discipline, self-responsibility are the triple safeguards of the independence of men.

Bernice Moore

Whatever your lot may be, paddle your own canoe.

Edward P. Philpots

The man who makes everything that leads to happiness depend upon himself, and not upon other men, has adopted the very best plan for living happily.

Plato

No one's happiness but my own is in my power to achieve or to destroy.

Ayn Rand

If someone betrays you once, it is his fault. If he betrays you twice, it is your fault.

Eleanor Roosevelt

We forfeit three-fourths of ourselves in order to be like other people.

Arthur Schopenhauer

Humanity is fortunate, because no man is unhappy except by his own fault.

Seneca

A great step towards independence is a good-humored stomach.

Seneca

While I am not in favor of maladjustment, I view this cultivation of neutrality, this breeding of mental neuters, this hostility to eccentricity and controversy with grave misgiving. One looks back with dismay at the possibility of a Shakespeare perfectly adjusted to bourgeois life in Stratford, a Wesley contentedly administering a country parish, George Washington going to London to receive a barony from George III, or Abraham Lincoln prospering in Springfield with nary a concern for the crumbling union.

Adlai Stevenson

The longer I live the more I realize the impact of attitude on life. Attitude, to me, is more than the past, than education, than money, than circumstances, than failures, than success, than what other people think or say or do. It is more important than appearance, giftedness, or skill. It will make or break an organization . . . a school . . . a home. The remarkable thing is we have a choice every day regarding the attitude we will embrace for that day. We cannot change our past. . . . We cannot change the fact that people will act in a certain way. We cannot change the inevitable. The only thing we can do is play on the one string we have. And that is our attitude. . . . I am convinced life is ten percent what happens to me and ninety percent how I react to it.

Charles Swindoll

Public opinion is a weak tyrant compared with our own private opinion. What a man thinks of himself, that it is which determines, or rather indicates, his fate.

Henry David Thoreau

Blessed are those who can please themselves.

Zulu proverb

The biggest mistake you can make is to believe that you work for someone else.

Unknown

We're all dysfunctional. Get over it.

Bumper sticker

Self-Leadership

According to the principle of self-leadership, members of a group are leaders by virtue of who they are and how they influence others, not by the positions they hold. They lead by example, through character and good judgment.

The influence of each human being on others in this life is a kind of immortality.

John Quincy Adams

We must become the change we wish to see in the world.

Mahatma Gandhi

I have never considered a difference of opinion in politics, in religion, in philosophy, as a cause for withdrawing from a friend.

Thomas Jefferson

No person is fit to command another that cannot command himself.

William Penn

If you conceal your secret from your friend, you deserve to lose him.

Portuguese proverb

Discretion is the better part of valor.

Unknown

Self-Sufficiency

These days, instead of taking emergency bivouac gear, guys go out on hard climbs and take nothing but a radio. If things get sketchy, they assume they can just get on the horn and call for a rescue.

John Bouchard

At altitude, supplemental oxygen makes it possible for an individual who is not prepared physically or mentally to step over the border of his own limits and to wander unaware in the Death Zone.

Anatoli Boukreev

Wealth consists not in having great possessions, but in having few wants.

Epicurus

It is usually easier and more reliable to carry extra tricks up your sleeve instead of extra gear in your pack.

John Gookin

Then came the gadgeteer, otherwise known as the sporting-goods dealer. He has draped the American outdoorsman with an infinity of contraptions, all offered as aids to self-reliance, hardihood, wood-craft, or marksmanship, but too often functioning as substitutes for them. Gadgets fill the pockets, they dangle from the neck and belt. The overflow fills the auto-trunk and also the trailer. Each item of outdoor equipment grows lighter and often better, but the aggregate poundage becomes tonnage.

Aldo Leopold
A Sand County Almanac

Equipment has little to do with the quality of the adventure. For that we ask: is there a bold line, uncertainty, objective danger, isolation, and the need for self-reliance?

Todd Thompson

We make ourselves rich by making our wants few.

Henry David Thoreau

The more you know, the less you need.

Unknown

Service

Service to a just cause rewards the worker with more real happiness and satisfaction than any other venture of life.

Carrie Chapman Catt

To devote a portion of one's leisure to doing something for someone else is one of the highest forms of recreation.

Gerald B. Fitzgerald

Service is the rent we pay for our room on earth.

Lord Halifax

I don't know what your destiny will be, but one thing I know: the only ones among you who will be really happy are those who will have sought and found how to serve.

Albert Schweitzer

The world has never been so rich in helpers as it is today, and consequently never have there been people so happy and so blessed in their lives. Volunteers for human service seem to spring from the ground. It would be difficult to point out a more encouraging fact for the world's future.

Minot Simms

Spirit

You don't get to choose how you're going to die. Or when. You can only decide how you're going to live. Now.

Joan Baez

Follow your bliss and don't be afraid, and doors will open where you didn't know they were going to be.

Joseph Campbell

To live is so startling it leaves time for little else.

Emily Dickinson

The mountains can be reached in all seasons. They offer a fighting challenge to heart, soul and mind, both in summer and winter. If throughout time the youth of the nation accept the challenge the mountains offer, they will keep alive in our people the spirit of adventure. That spirit is a measure of the vitality of both nations and men. A people who climb the ridges and sleep under the stars in high mountain meadows, who enter the forest and scale peaks, who explore glaciers and walk ridges buried deep in snow—these people will give their country some of the indomitable spirit of the mountains.

William O. Douglas

Anticipate the good so that you may enjoy it.

Ethiopian proverb

To know is nothing at all; to imagine is everything.

Anatole France

Liberty is a thing of the spirit—to be free to worship, to think, to hold opinions, and to speak without fear, free to challenge wrong and oppression with surety of justice.

Herbert Hoover

The sovereign invigorator of the body is exercise.

Thomas Jefferson

Life is either a daring adventure or nothing.

Helen Keller

Life is short—live it up.

Nikita Khrushchev

A man's best moments seem to go by before he notices them; and he spends a large part of his life reaching back for them, like a runner for a baton that will never come.

David Roberts

Morale is increased by the accomplishment of difficult tasks.

Erwin Rommel

Life has to be lived. That's all there is to it.

Eleanor Roosevelt

Our life is frittered away by detail. . . . Simplify, simplify.

Henry David Thoreau
Walden

If you can spend a perfectly useless afternoon in a perfectly useless manner, you have learned how to live.

Lin Yutang

If you can walk, you can dance. If you can talk, you can sing.

Zimbabwean proverb

Above all, life should be fun.

Unknown

Spirituality

*One definition of spirituality is the recognition of connections and
relationships and their meaning. Both the outdoor environment and
human community are fertile places for awareness of these connections. Spirituality can include "organized" religion, but it is
easily discussed and experienced without depending on a single religious tradition, or any at all.*

To live content with small means,
to seek elegance rather than luxury,
and refinement rather than fashion,
to be worthy, not respectable, and wealthy, not rich.
To study hard, think quietly, talk gently, act frankly,
to listen to stars and birds, babes and sages, with open
       heart,
to bear all cheerfully,
do all bravely,
await occasions,
hurry never—
in a word, to let the spiritual, unbidden and unconscious,
grow up through the common.
This is to be my symphony.

William Ellery Channing

What is life? It is the flash of a firefly in the night. It is the breath of a
buffalo in the winter time. It is the little shadow which runs across
the grass and loses itself in the Sunset.

Crowfoot of the Blackfoot Nation, on his deathbed

Any religion is good if it results in more ethical behavior.

The Dalai Lama

What avail is it to win prescribed amounts of information about geography and history, to win the ability to read and write, if in the process the individual loses his own soul; loses his appreciation of things worthwhile, of the values to which these are related; if he loses the desire to apply what he has learned, and above all, loses the ability to extract meaning from his future experiences as they occur?

John Dewey

We need not be afraid of the future, for the future will be in our own hands. We shall need courage, energy, and determination, but above all, we shall need faith—faith in ourselves, in our communities, and in our country.

Thomas E. Dewey

What I see in Nature is a magnificent structure that we can comprehend only very imperfectly, and that must fill a thinking person with a feeling of humility. This is a genuinely religious feeling that has nothing to do with mysticism.

Albert Einstein

The only thing we really have is now. Widen our circles of compassion to embrace all living creatures and the whole of nature in its beauty.

Albert Einstein

Everyone who is seriously involved in the pursuit of science becomes convinced that a spirit is manifest in the laws of the Universe—a spirit vastly superior to that of man, and one in the face of which we with our modest powers must feel humble.

Albert Einstein

The cosmic religious experience is the strongest and noblest driving force behind scientific research.

Albert Einstein

If the possibility of the spiritual development of all individuals is to be secured, a second kind of outward freedom is necessary. The development of science and of the creative activities of the spirit in general requires still another kind of freedom, which may be characterised as inward freedom. It is this freedom of the spirit which consists in the interdependence of thought from the restrictions of authoritarian and social prejudices as well as from unphilosophical routinizing and habit in general. This inward freedom is an infrequent gift of nature and a worthy object for the individual.

Albert Einstein

The most beautiful emotion we can experience is the mysterious. It is the power of all true art and science. He to whom this emotion is a stranger, who can no longer wonder and stand rapt in awe, is as good as dead. To know that what is impenetrable in us really exists, manifesting itself as the highest wisdom and the most radiant beauty, which our dull faculties can comprehend only in their most primitive forms—this knowledge, this feeling, is at the center of true religiousness.

Albert Einstein
speech to the German League of Human Rights

The fairest thing we can experience is the mysterious. It is the fundamental emotion which stands at the cradle of true art and true science.

Albert Einstein

I have loved climbing, and the reason is that if you are up there and having a beautiful day and everyone is clicking and a few cumulus clouds are sprinkled around and everyone is moving and handling the rope right and the air is clean and you can see forever, well, I think that is almost an unmatchable experience. It is almost sacred.

Glenn Exum

Only a person who has faith in himself can be faithful to others.

Erich Fromm

It's not your religion if you only do it in church.

John Gookin

I think over again my small adventures
my fears
those small ones that seemed so big
for all the vital things
I had to get and to reach.
And yet there is only one great thing
the only thing
to live to see the great day that dawns
and the light that fills the world.

Inuit song
Never Cry Wolf

I think I was a little drunk on the air up there, but it was beautiful being on top. Vague and indistinct, fabled peaks rose out of the ice and rock below.

Shari Kearny

I was going [mountaineering] again because I had need of courage and inspiration and because on the high mountains I find them as nowhere else.

Dora Keen

Prayer does not change God, but changes one who prays.

Søren Kierkegaard

Love is the supreme unifying principle of life.

Martin Luther King, Jr.

The land is like poetry: it is inexplicably coherent, it is transcendent in its meaning, and it has the power to elevate a consideration of human life.

Barry Lopez

The great omission in American life is solitude; not loneliness, for this is an alienation that thrives most in the midst of crowds, but that zone of time and space free from outside pressure which is the incubator of the spirit.

Marya Mannes

Central to White Buffalo Woman's message, to all native spirituality, is the understanding that the Great Spirit lives in all things, enlivens all forms, and gives energy to all things in all realms of creation, including earthly life. . . . Ancient teachings call us to turn primary attention to the Sacred Web Of Life, of which we are a part and with which we are so obviously entangled. This quality of attention—of paying attention to the whole—is called among my people "holiness."

Brooke Medicine Eagle of the Crow Nation

We can never have enough of nature. We must be refreshed by the sight of inexhaustible vigor, vast and titanic features.

John Muir

Thousands of tired, nerve-shaken, over-civilized people are beginning to find out that going to the mountains is going home; that wilderness is a necessity; that mountain parks and reservations are useful not only as fountains of timber and irrigating rivers, but as fountains of life.

John Muir

There are many people who look upon mountaineering adventures and activities as a preposterous waste of human energy, involving unnecessary risks to life and limb. They are entitled to their opinion and may be left to lead their comfortable lives and to die in a bed. The fact remains that there are other men who feel an urge to the high places, men whose spiritual natures are drawn to them, irresistibly, and who there gain the spiritual sustenance their souls crave.

John Noel
The Story of Everest

The seat of the soul is there where the inner world and outer world meet.

Novalis

Compassion emerges from a sense of belonging: the experience that all suffering is like our suffering and all joy is like our joy. When we know ourselves to be connected to all others, acting compassionately is simply the natural thing to do.

True compassion requires us to attend to our own humanity, to come to a deep acceptance of our own life as it is. It requires us to come into right relationship with that which is most human in ourselves, that which is most capable of suffering.

By recognizing and attending to that basic humanness, our basic human integrity, we find the place of profound connection to all life. That connection then becomes for us the ground of being. It is only through connection that we can recover true compassion, or any sense of authentic meaning in life: a sense of the mysterious, the profound, the sacred nature of the world.

Rachel Naomi Remen
The Heart of Learning

On the path that leads to Nowhere I have sometimes found my Soul.

Corrine Roosevelt Robins

There is a delight in the hardy life of the open. There are no words that can tell the hidden spirit of the wilderness, that can reveal its mystery, its melancholy and its charm.

Theodore Roosevelt

Let a man once begin to think about the mystery of his life and the links which connect him with the life that fills the world, and he cannot but bring to bear upon his own life and all other life that comes within his reach the principle of reverence for life.

Albert Schweitzer

No ray of sunlight is ever lost, but the green which it awakes into existence needs time to sprout, and it is not always granted to the sower to see the harvest. All work that is worth anything is done in faith.

Albert Schweitzer

The springs of enchantment lie within ourselves; they arise from our sense of wonder, that most precious of gifts, the birthright of every child.

Eric Shipton

If I had my life to live over again, I'd try to make more mistakes next time. I would relax. I would limber up. I would be sillier than I have been this trip. I know of very few things I would take seriously. I would be crazier. I would be less hygienic. I would take more chances. I would take more trips. I would climb more mountains, swim more rivers, and watch more sunsets. I would burn more gasoline. I would eat more ice cream and fewer beans. I would have more actual problems and fewer imaginary ones.

You see, I am one of those people who live prophylactically and sensibly, and sanely. Hour after hour. Day by day. Oh, I have had my moments, and if I had it to do over again, I'd have more of them. In fact, I'd have nothing else. Just moments, one right after another, instead of living so many years ahead of each day. I have been one of those people who never go anywhere without a thermometer, a hot water bottle, a gargle, a raincoat, and a parachute. If I had it to do over again, I would go places and do things, and travel lighter than I have. If I had my life to live over, I would start barefoot earlier in the spring and stay that way later in the fall. I would play hooky more often. I wouldn't make good grades except by accident. I would ride more merry-go-rounds. I'd pick more daisies.

Attributed to Nadine Stair; adapted from an essay by Don Herold

When humans participate in ceremony, they enter sacred space. Everything outside of that space shrivels in importance. Time takes on a different dimension. Emotions flow more freely. The bodies of participants become filled with the energy of life, and this energy reaches out and blesses the creation around them. All is made new; everything becomes sacred.

Sun Bear

The key to mountaineering spirit is not hard to find. . . . It lies not in what men *do*, but what they *are*—in the raising of their eyes and the lifting of their hearts.

James Ramsey Ullman
High Conquest

The mountains have done the spiritual side of me more good religiously, as well as in my body physically, than anything else in the world. No one knows who and what God is until he has seen some real mountaineering and climbing in the Alps.

Rev. F. T. Wethered
letter to the Alpine Journal, 1919

It isn't until you come to a spiritual understanding of who you are— not necessarily a religious feeling, but deep down, the spirit within— that you can begin to take control.

Oprah Winfrey

Stewardship

Stewardship in general is the careful and responsible management of something. As it relates to the wilderness, the philosophy of stewardship holds that it is our responsibility as a species to act as caretakers for the natural world and its resources.

One final paragraph of advice: Do not burn yourselves out. Be as I am—a reluctant enthusiast . . . a part-time crusader, a half-hearted fanatic. Save the other half of yourselves and your lives for pleasure and adventure. It is not enough to fight for the land; it is even more important to enjoy it. While you can. While it's still there. So get out there and hunt and fish and mess around with your friends, ramble out yonder and explore the forests, encounter the grizz, climb the mountains, bag the peaks, run the rivers, breathe deep of that yet sweet and lucid air, sit quietly for a while and contemplate the precious stillness, that lovely, mysterious and awesome space. Enjoy yourselves, keep your brain in your head and your head firmly attached to the body, the body active and alive, and I promise you this much: I promise you this one sweet victory over our enemies, over those deskbound people with their hearts in a safe deposit box and their eyes hypnotized by desk calculators. I promise you this: you will outlive the bastards.

Edward Abbey, at a 1987 Earth First! rally

In losing stewardship we lose fellowship; we become outcasts from the great neighborhood of creation.

Wendell Berry
The Gift of Good Land

Pick battles big enough to matter, small enough to win.

Jonathan Kozol

There are no passengers on spaceship earth. We are all crew.

Marshall McLuhan

Taking Risks

A venturesome minority will always be eager to set off on their own, and no obstacles should be placed in their path; let them take risks, for Godsake, let them get lost, sunburnt, stranded, drowned, eaten by bears, buried alive under avalanches. That is the right and privilege of any free American.

Edward Abbey
Desert Solitaire

The early bird catches the worm. But the second mouse usually gets the cheese.

American folk saying

I think we should follow a simple rule: if we can take the worst, take the risk.

Joyce Brothers

It is not Justice the servant of men, but accident, hazard, Fortune—the ally of patient Time—that holds an even and scrupulous balance.

Joseph Conrad

Paying very close attention to your intuition is perhaps the most important rule of all. If I am distracted by doubt or fear, I don't do it.

Lynn Hill

Mistakes are part of the dues one pays for a full life.

Sophia Loren

Take calculated risks. That is quite different from being rash.

George Patton

Too much caution is bad for you. By avoiding things you fear, you may let yourself in for unhappy consequences. It is usually wiser to stand up to a scary-seeming experience and walk right into it, risking the bruises and hard knocks. You are likely to find it is not as tough as you had thought. Or you may find it plenty tough, but also discover you have what it takes to handle it.

Norman Vincent Peale

I compensate for big risks by always doing my homework and being well-prepared. I can take on larger risks by reducing the overall risk.

Donna Shalala

People are the massive variable. I go with one person who is basically made of granite. You want someone who is watching out for you to a degree you never question.

Todd Skinner

In time of peace in the modern world, if one is thoughtful and quiet, it is [more] difficult to be killed or maimed in the outland places of the globe than it is in the streets of our great cities, but the atavistic urge towards danger persists and its satisfaction is called adventure.

John Steinbeck
Log from the Sea of Cortez

The secret of my success is that I always managed to live to fly another day.

Chuck Yeager

I believe that courage is all too often mistakenly seen as the absence of fear. If you descend by ropes from a cliff and are not fearful to some degree, you are either crazy or unaware. Courage is seeing your fear, in a realistic perspective, defining it, considering alternatives, and choosing to function in spite of risks.

Leonard Zunk

To laugh is to risk appearing the fool. To weep is to risk appearing sentimental. To reach out for another is to risk involvement. To expose feelings is to risk exposing your true self. To place your ideas, your dreams before the crowd is to risk their loss. To love is to risk not being loved in return. To live is to risk dying. To hope is to risk despair. To try is to risk failure. But risks must be taken, because the greatest hazard in life is to risk nothing. The person who risks nothing does nothing, has nothing, and is nothing. He may avoid suffering and sorrow, but he simply cannot learn, feel, change, grow, love—live. Chained by his certitudes, he is a slave, he has forfeited freedom. Only a person who risks is free.

Unknown

Teamwork

Nothing is more dangerous than an idea when it is the only one you have.

Emile Auguste Chartier

Between the five of us was the strong bond of the sea, and also the fellowship of the craft, which no amount of enthusiasm for yachting, cruising or so on can give, since one is only the amusement of life and the other is life itself.

Joseph Conrad

It is not so much our friend's help that helps as the confidence of their help.

Epicurus

Coming together is a beginning; keeping together is progress; working together is success.

Henry Ford

Together we knew toil, joy and pain. My fervent wish is that the nine of us who were united in the face of death should remain fraternally united through life.

Maurice Herzog

When the pursuit of natural harmony is a shared journey, great heights can be attained.

Lynn Hill

None of us are as smart as all of us.

Japanese proverb

Now this is the Law of the Jungle—as old and as true as
the sky;
And the Wolf that shall keep it may prosper, but the
Wolf that shall break it must die.
As the creeper that girdles the tree-trunk, the Law
runneth forward and back—
For the strength of the Pack is the Wolf, and the strength
of the Wolf is the Pack.

Rudyard Kipling
The Second Jungle Book

Individual commitment to a group effort—that is what makes a team work, a company work, a society work, a civilization work.

Vince Lombardi

The greatest service we can perform for others is to help them to help themselves.

Horace Mann

If everyone is thinking alike then someone isn't thinking.

George Patton

If you want a track team to win the high jump, you find one person who can jump seven feet, not seven people who can jump one foot.

Louis Terman

It is amazing what you can accomplish if you do not care who gets the credit.

Harry Truman

Nothing motivates a person more than to see his boss putting in an honest day's work.

From *Wain's Conclusions*

Tolerance for Adversity

Worry is evidence of an ill-controlled brain; it is merely a stupid waste of time in unpleasantness. If men and women practiced mental calisthenics, they would purge their brains of this foolishness.

Arnold Bennett

I've never been one who thought the good Lord should make life easy; I've just asked him to make me strong.

Eva Bowring

Perhaps one has to be very old before one learns how to be amused
rather than shocked.

Pearl S. Buck

If you are patient in one moment of anger, you will escape a hundred
days of sorrow.

Chinese proverb

As a cure for worrying, work is far better than whiskey.

Thomas Edison

People's perceptions of comfort often change as they spend more and
more time out camping. The cold becomes less cold, the hot less hot,
and the mosquitoes less annoying. It is not a matter of being tough
and taking it. Rather it seems as though reality gradually redefines
itself until you are comfortable with less.

Thomas Elpel
Participating in Nature

There is only one way to happiness, and that is to cease worrying
about things which are beyond the power of our will.

Epictetus

Education is the ability to listen to almost anything without losing
your temper or your self-confidence.

Robert Frost

You'll break the worry habit the day you decide you can meet and
master the worst that can happen to you.

Arnold Glasow

Don't let other people's poor planning turn into your crisis.

John Gookin

That which we persist in doing becomes easier for us to do. Not that
the nature of the thing is changed, but that our power to do is increased.

Heber J. Grant

Your disability is your opportunity.

Kurt Hahn

When the morning's freshness has been replaced by the weariness of mid-day, when the leg muscles quiver under the strain, the climb seems endless, and, suddenly, nothing will go quite as you wish—it is then that you must not hesitate.

Dag Hammarskjold

Do not handicap your children by making their lives easy.

Robert Heinlein

In overstepping our limitations, in touching the extreme boundaries of man's world, we have come to know something of its true splendor. In my worst moments of anguish, I seemed to discover the deep significance of existence which till then I had been unawares. I saw that it was better to be true than to be strong. The marks of the ordeal are apparent on my body. I was saved and I had won my freedom. This freedom, which I shall never lose, has given me the assurance and serenity of a man who has fulfilled himself.

Maurice Herzog
Annapurna

The true test of character is not how much we know how to do, but how we behave when we don't know what to do.

John Holt

Nothing gives one person so much advantage over another as to remain cool and unruffled under all circumstances.

Thomas Jefferson

I find that the harder I work, the more luck I seem to have.

Thomas Jefferson

Keep your face to the sunshine and you cannot see the shadows.

Helen Keller

The ultimate measure of a man is not where he stands in moments of comfort, but where he stands at times of challenge and controversy.

Martin Luther King, Jr.

He who wants to have right without wrong, order without disorder, does not understand the principles of heaven and earth. He does not know how things hang together. Can man cling only to heaven and know nothing of earth?

Lao Tzu

Are you going to let that ruin your *whole* day?

Marine saying

The life force is vigorous. The delight that accompanies it counter-balances all the pains and hardships that confront men.

W. Somerset Maugham

Worry compounds the futility of being trapped on a dead-end street. Thinking opens new avenues.

Charles W. Mayo

God grant me the serenity to accept the things I cannot change, the courage to change the things I can, and the wisdom to know the difference.

Reinhold Niebuhr

If you want the rainbow, you gotta put up with the rain.

Dolly Parton

The mark of a great fighter is how he acts when he is getting licked.

Sugar Ray Robinson

When you get to the end of your rope, tie a knot and hang on.

Franklin D. Roosevelt

The problem is not that there are problems. The problem is expecting otherwise and thinking that having problems is a problem.

Theodore Rubin

To act coolly, intelligently and prudently in perilous circumstances is the test of a man and also of a nation.

Adlai Stevenson

If you want a place in the sun, you've got to put up with a few blisters.

Abigail Van Buren

Life is thickly sown with thorns, and I know no other remedy than to pass quickly through them. The longer we dwell on our misfortunes, the greater is their power to harm us.

Voltaire

The greater part of our happiness or misery depends on our dispositions and not on our circumstances.

Martha Washington

Extreme cold when it first arrives seems to generate cheerfulness and sociability. For a few hours all life's dubious problems are dropped in favor of the clear and congenial task of keeping alive.

E. B. White

There was a time when meadow, grove, and stream,
The earth, and every common sight,
To me did seem
Apparelled in celestial light,
The glory and the freshness of a dream.
It is not now as it hath been of yore;—
Turn wheresoe'er I may,
By night or day,
The things which I have seen I now can see no more. . . .

Though nothing can bring back the hour
Of splendour in the grass, of glory in the flower;

We will grieve not, rather find
Strength in what remains behind.

William Wordsworth
*from "Ode: Intimations of Immortality from
Recollections of Early Childhood"*

Your trials did not come to punish you, but to awaken you.

Paramahansa Yogananda

If you understand, then things are just as they are. If you do not
understand, then things are just as they are.

Zen verse

Lunch never tasted so good. I am awash with a sense of well-being,
of joy in living, of being here, at this time, this place—a quart of
water, some protein, a little fat, and a lot of salt, and my body
responds gratefully and my spirits soar right into euphoria.

For most of the time, one disciplines oneself to ignore the
discomfort of being hot or tired or having sore hip bones or swollen
hands or being hungry, thirsty, or all together all at once. I may write
about them later but at the time they are simply set aside, and it is
probably this ignoring of basic misery that makes a backpacker.
Someone once characterized backpacking as the most miserable way
he could think of of getting from point A to point B. I wouldn't go
that far, but I do know that if you stopped to inventory where you
hurt, you likely would not continue, having discovered that you are
not only a masochist but a fool as well. But when salt restores the
electrolytic balance, when water cools the insides as well as the
brow, when food refurbishes the body's cells, when time has been
spent off one's feet and a heavy pack is a mile downcanyon, then
there follows a tremendous rush of well-being, a physical sense of
buoyancy, all out of proportion to the time and place.

Ann Zwinger
Wind in the Rock: The Canyonlands of Southeastern Utah

Nothing is particularly hard if you divide it into small jobs.

Unknown

Vision and Action

Words are a form of action, capable of influencing change. Their articulation represents a complete, lived experience.

Ingrid Bengis

Managers are people who do things right, while leaders are people who do the right thing.

Warren Bennis
On Becoming a Leader

Leadership is the capacity to translate vision into reality.

Warren Bennis

All that is necessary for the triumph of evil is that good men do nothing.

Edmund Burke

We write our own destiny. We become what we do.

Madame Chiang Kai-shek

Talk does not cook rice.

Chinese proverb

A man must sit in a chair with his mouth open for very long time before a roast duck flies in.

Chinese proverb

To see what is right, and not do it, is want of courage, or of principle.

Confucius

One never notices what has been done; one can only see what remains to be done.

Marie Curie

Perfection of means and confusion of ends seems—in my opinion—to characterize our age.

Albert Einstein

Imagination is more important than knowledge.

Albert Einstein

The world belongs to the energetic.

Ralph Waldo Emerson

No man is able to make progress when he is wavering between opposite things.

Epictetus

Always dream and shoot higher than you know you can do. Don't bother just to be better than your contemporaries or predecessors. Try to be better than yourself.

William Faulkner

Well done is better than well said.

Benjamin Franklin

Up, sluggard, and waste not life; in the grave will be sleeping enough.

Benjamin Franklin

The purpose of life is to believe, to hope, and to strive.

Indira Gandhi

Whatever you can do, or dream you can, begin it.
Boldness has genius, power, magic in it.
Attributed to Johann Wolfgang von Goethe

Knowing is not enough; we must apply.
Willing is not enough; we must do.
Johann Wolfgang von Goethe

Idealists, foolish enough to throw caution to the winds, have
advanced humankind and have enriched the world.

Emma Goldman

There's a fine line between perseverance and obstinacy.

John Gookin

Mediocrity obtains more with application than superiority without it.

Baltasar Gracian

Nothing is more revealing than movement.

Martha Graham

Never confuse motion with action.

Ernest Hemingway

Life is to be lived. If you have to support yourself, you had bloody
well better find some way that is going to be interesting. And you
don't do that by sitting around wondering about yourself.

Katharine Hepburn

It is not enough to aim. You must hit.

Italian proverb

Whenever you are to do a thing, though it can never be known but to
yourself, ask yourself how you would act were all the world looking
at you, and act accordingly.

Thomas Jefferson

I am only one; but I am still one. I cannot do everything, but still I
can do something. I will not refuse to do the something I can do.

Helen Keller

Science may have found a cure for most evils; but it has found no
remedy for the worst of them all—the apathy of human beings.

Helen Keller

No pessimist ever discovered the secrets of the stars, or sailed to an uncharted land, or opened a new heaven to the human spirit.

Helen Keller

We will be known by the tracks we leave behind.

Lakota proverb

Leadership is action, not position.

Donald H. McGannon

Lord, grant that I might always desire more than I can accomplish.

Michelangelo

If I have seen further than others, it is because I have stood on the shoulders of giants.

Isaac Newton

Whether our efforts are or are not favored by life, let us be able to say, when we come near to the great goal, I have done what I could.

Louis Pasteur

Even if you're on the right track, you'll get run over if you just sit there.

Will Rogers

Keep your eyes on the stars and your feet on the ground.

Theodore Roosevelt

While we are postponing, life speeds by.

Seneca

It had long since come to my attention that people of accomplishment rarely sat back and let things happen to them. They went out and happened to things.

Elinor Smith

Better to do a little well than a great deal badly.

Socrates

Certainly a leader needs a clear vision of the organization and where it is going, but a vision is of little value unless it is shared in a way so as to generate enthusiasm and commitment. Leadership and communication are inseparable.

Claude I. Taylor

It is not enough to be busy. The question is: What are we busy about?

Henry David Thoreau

If one advances confidently in the direction of his dreams, and endeavors to live the life which he has imagined, he will meet with a success unexpected in common hours.

Henry David Thoreau

If you have built castles in the air, your work need not be lost; that is where they should be. Now put the foundations under them.

Henry David Thoreau

Few things are harder to put up with than the annoyance of a good example.

Mark Twain

Dreams are like the rudder of a ship setting sail. The rudder may be small and unseen, but it controls the ship's course.

Kim Woo-choong

Rust never sleeps.

Neil Young

A vision without a task is but a dream; a task without a vision is drudgery; a vision and a task is the hope of the world.

Inscription on a church in Sussex, England

Wilderness and Environmental Education

All who have meditated on the art of governing humankind have been convinced that the fate of empires depends on the education of youth.

Aristotle

Things do change. The only question is since things are deteriorating so quickly, will society and man's habits change quickly enough?

Isaac Asimov

The eye of the understanding is like the eye of the sense; for as you may see great objects through small crannies or holes, so you may see great axioms of nature through small and contemptible instances.

Francis Bacon

Education makes a people easy to lead, but difficult to drive; easy to govern, but impossible to enslave.

Henry Brougham

It is not half so important to *know* as to *feel*. If facts are the seeds that later produce knowledge and wisdom, then the emotions and the impressions of the senses are the fertile soil in which the seeds must grow.

Rachel Carson

Teachers open the door, but you must enter by yourself.

Chinese proverb

Poor is the pupil who does not surpass his master.

Leonardo da Vinci

One's work may be finished someday, but one's education, never.

Alexander Dumas

Good teaching is one-fourth preparation and three-fourths theater.

Gail Godwin

The ecologization of politics requires us to acknowledge the priority of universal human values and make ecology part of education and instruction from an early age, molding a new, modern approach to nature and, at the same time, giving back to man a sense of being a part of nature. No moral improvement of society is possible without that.

Mikhail Gorbachev

The two basic processes of education are knowing and valuing.

Robert J. Havighurst

There is a fitness in natural experience, an intimacy that may not be superceded. How many, in this world of devices, now live through the lifetime of tides, nights of clean wind and clear stars above the rooflines, know the genuine exposure to cold rain, cold water, and stiff fingers, and know how to be steady there?

John Hay

Speak to the earth and it will teach thee.

Job 12:8

The control man has secured over nature has far outrun his control over himself.

Ernest Jones

One looks back with appreciation to the brilliant teachers, but with gratitude to those who touch our human feelings. The curriculum is so much necessary raw material, but warmth is the vital element for the growing plant and for the soul of a child.

Carl Jung

Man always kills the things he loves, and so we the pioneers have killed the wilderness. Some say we had to. Be that as it may, I am glad I shall never be young without wild country to be young in. Of what avail are forty freedoms without a blank spot on the map?

Aldo Leopold
A Sand County Almanac

I am trying to teach you that this alphabet of "natural objects" (soils and rivers, birds and beasts) spells out a story. . . . Once you learn how to read the land, I have no fear of what you will do to it, or with it. And I know many pleasant things it will do to you.

Aldo Leopold
The River of the Mother of God and Other Essays

The objective is to teach the student to see the land, to understand what he sees, and enjoy what he understands.

Aldo Leopold

From the top of a hill . . . I gained the last wistful, lingering view of the beautiful university grounds and buildings. . . . I bade my blessed alma mater farewell. But I was only leaving one university for another, the Wisconsin University for the University of the Wilderness.

John Muir

Every one of these techniques that we teach . . . we can teach conservation right along with it. This is the place, when we're fishing, to teach about the relations of the fish to the ecology and how we can keep fishing these lakes and streams and not fish them out. We go to lakes that are overpopulated where actually fishing becomes a public service to catch some of the fish out so the others can grow larger and fatter.

Paul Petzoldt

The future of humankind, peace, progress, and prosperity must be finally determined by the extent to which men can be brought to a state of common and honest understanding.

Ralph C. Smedley

I went to the woods because I wished to live deliberately, to confront only the essential facts of life, and see if I could not learn what it had to teach, and not, when I came to die, discover that I had not lived. . . . I wanted to live deep and suck out all the marrow of life, to live so sturdily and Spartan-like as to put to rout all that was not life, to cut a broad swath and shave close, to drive life into a corner, and reduce it to its lowest terms.

Henry David Thoreau
Walden

In wildness is the preservation of the earth.

Henry David Thoreau

An infallible method of making fanatics is to persuade before you instruct.

Voltaire

Education is not the filling of a pail, but the lighting of a fire.

William Butler Yeats

No one cares how much you know until they know how much you care.

Unknown

The Wilderness Experience

If one is inclined to wonder at first how so many dwellers came to be in the loneliest land that ever came out of God's hands, what they do there and why stay, one does not wonder so much after having lived there. None but this long brown land lays such a hold on the affections.

Mary Austin

To move among other great forms of life existing free of us is to be able to sense a wisdom different from and perhaps greater than our own.

Tom Bender

And there at the camp we had around us the elemental world of water and light, and earth and air. We felt the presences of the wild creatures, the river, the trees, the stars. Though we had our troubles, we had them in a true perspective. The universe, as we could see any night, is unimaginably large, and mostly dark. We knew we needed to be together more than we needed to be apart.

Wendell Berry

Do nothing. Time is too precious to waste.

Buddha

Why go into the wilderness? The natural world can be hard work, frustrating and uncomfortable, but we go nonetheless. What pulls us there, to a place that we may perceive as unwelcoming? For me, and maybe you too, there is a very real tugging at the soul, a deep-rooted desire to find something, to achieve something, a metaphysical fix of some sort.

The oppressive influences of our modern society keep many of us from being our real selves. We continually react not to Mother Nature, but to Mother Culture, and we take on identities and personalities not our own. But when we step into the wilderness, we temporarily liberate ourselves from those influences. Perhaps we begin to discover a little more about our real selves. Maybe we'll get some reassurance there is something behind it all, and that it's good.

I spend up to thirty days at a time in the wilderness, instructing for an outdoor school, and many of my fellow travelers are new to the Grand Experience of wilderness travel. They'll often excitedly vocalize their observation: "We are in the middle of *nowhere*!"; "There is *nothing* out here!"; "Y'know, back in the *real* world. . . ."

I have learned that it's impossible to be nowhere, much less in the middle of it. Wherever you are, and most especially the wilderness, you are—quite definitely—*somewhere*.

In the backcountry, you are surrounded, not by nothing, but by lots and lots of something, an amazing variety of the interlocking *everything*!

Don't look away over the distant horizon for some place called the real world. That is the illusion. Wherever you are, any place your feet are planted on this fabulously complex and beautiful Earth, you are most assuredly in the real world.

Mike Clelland

We go to sanctuaries to remember the things we hold most dear, the things we cherish and love. And then—our greatest challenge—we return home seeking to enact this wisdom as best we can in our daily lives.

William Cronan

The wilderness is a place of rest—not in the sense of being motionless, for the lure, after all, is to move, to round the next bend. The rest comes in the isolation from distractions, in the slowing of the daily centrifugal forces that keep us off balance.

David Douglas

To be whole and harmonious, man must also know the music of the beaches and the woods. He must find the thing of which he is only an infinitesimal part and nurture it and love it, if he is to live.

William O. Douglas

Life is good only when it is magical and musical, a perfect timing and consent, and when we do not anatomise it. . . . You must hear the bird's song without attempting to render it into nouns and verbs.

Ralph Waldo Emerson
Society and Solitude

There is more to life than increasing its speed.

Mahatma Gandhi

The essence of pleasure is spontaneity.

Germaine Greer

There is a great deal of talk these days about saving the environment. We must, for the environment sustains our bodies. But as humans we also require support for our spirits, and this is what certain kinds of places provide. The catalyst that converts any physical location . . . into a place is the process of experiencing deeply. A place is a piece of the whole environment that has been claimed by feelings. Viewed simply as a life-support system, the earth is an environment. Viewed as a resource that sustains our humanity, the earth is a collection of places. We never speak, for example, of an environment we have known; it is always places we have known—and recall. We are homesick for places, we are reminded of places, it is the sounds and smells and sights of places which haunt us and against which we often measure our present.

Alan Gussow
A Sense of Place

Well, we knocked the bastard off.

Edmund Hillary

Something of our personality has gone into every mountain on which we have spent our strength and on which our thoughts have rested, and something of its personality has come into ours and had its small effect on everything that has come within our influence.

R. L. G. Irving

Look to this day! For it is life, the very life of life. In its brief course lie all the verities and realities of your existence; the bliss of growth, the glory of action, the splendor of beauty. For yesterday is but a dream and tomorrow is only a vision, but today well lived makes every yesterday a dream of happiness and every tomorrow a vision of hope. Look well, therefore, to this day! Such is the salutation of the dawn.

Omar Khayyam
Listen to the Exhortation of the Dawn

In wilderness I sense the miracle of life, and behind it our scientific accomplishments fade to trivia.

Charles Lindbergh

It has done me good to be somewhat parched by the heat and
drenched by the rain of life.

Henry Wadsworth Longfellow

For a relationship with landscape to be lasting, it must be reciprocal.
At the level at which the land supplies our food, this is not difficult to
comprehend, and the mutuality is often recalled in a grace at meals.
At the level at which landscape seems beautiful or frightening to us
and leaves us affected, or at the level at which it furnishes us with
metaphors and symbols with which we pry into mystery, the nature
of reciprocity is harder to define. In approaching the land with an
attitude of obligation, willing to observe courtesies difficult to articulate—perhaps only a gesture of the hands—one establishes a regard
from which dignity can emerge. From that dignified relationship with
the land, it is possible to imagine an extension of dignified relationships throughout one's life. Each relationship is formed of the same
integrity, which initially makes the mind say: the things in the land fit
together perfectly, even though they are always changing. I wish the
order of my life to be arranged in the same way I find the light, the
slight movement of the wind, the voice of a bird, the heading of a
seed pod I see before me. This impeccable and indisputable integrity
I want for myself.

Barry Lopez
Arctic Dreams

You can't take a crash course in serenity.

Shirley MacLaine

For me, and for thousands with similar inclinations, the most important passion of life is the overpowering desire to escape periodically
from the clutches of a mechanistic civilization. To us the enjoyment
of solitude, complete independence, and the beauty of undefiled
panoramas is absolutely essential to happiness.

Bob Marshall

I'd rather wake up in the middle of nowhere than in any city on earth.

Steve McQueen

It is the enjoying, not the possessing, that makes us happy.

Michelangelo

A poetic appreciation of life, combined with a knowledge of nature, creates humility, which in turn becomes the greatness of man.

Olaus Murie

The smaller we come to feel ourselves compared to the mountain, the nearer we come to participating in its greatness. I do not know why this is so.

Arne Naess

The Wilderness holds answers to questions man has not yet learned how to ask.

Nancy Newhall

I seem always to enjoy things more intensely because of the certainty that they will not last.

Everett Ruess

One of the best-paying professions is getting ahold of pieces of country in your mind, learning their smell and their moods, sorting out the pieces of a view, deciding what grows here and there and why, how many steps that hill will take, where this creek winds and where it meets the other one below, what elevation timberline is now, whether you can walk this reef at low tide or have to climb around, which contour lines on a map mean better cliffs or mountains. This is the best kind of ownership, and the most permanent.

It feels good to say, "I know the Sierra," or, "I know Point Reyes." But of course you don't—what you know better is yourself, and Point Reyes and the Sierra have helped.

Terry and Renny Russell
On the Loose

Fond as we are of our loved ones, there comes at times during their absence an unexplained peace.

Anne Shaw

The hills not only take men away from a complex mode of existence, but teach them to be happy it is only necessary to have food, a shelter and warmth. They bring them face to face with realities, and in doing so inculcate a valuable lesson in the association of simplicity and happiness.

For these reasons any development that tends to bring [men] into close touch with the natural order of things is a value to mankind, inasmuch as it helps them to gain a sense of proportion. It is impossible for any thinking man to look down from a hill onto a crowded plain and ponder over the relative importance of things. To take a simple view is to take a wider view. Whatever our beliefs, whatever our creeds from which we seek to extract happiness when we live on the plain, we find that things that have puzzled us are made clear when we stand on a hill. On a hill we are content to be content.

And so from the hills we return refreshed in body, in mind and in spirit, to grapple anew with life's problems. For a while we have lived simply, wisely and happily; we have made good friends; we have adventured well.

Frank S. Smythe

Our growth depends not on how many experiences we devour, but on how many we digest.

Ralph W. Sockman

This stillness, solitude, wildness of nature is a kind of thoroughwort or boneset, to my intellect. This is what I go out to seek. It is as if I always met in those places some grand, serene, immortal, infinitely encouraging though invisible, companion, and walked with him.

Henry David Thoreau

And so what is the final test of the efficacy of this wilderness experience we've just been through together? Because having been there, in the mountains, alone, in the midst of solitude, and this feeling, this mystical feeling if you will, of the ultimacy of joy and whatever there is. The questions is, "Why not stay out there in the wilderness the rest of your days and just live in the lap of satori (a state of intuitive illumination) or whatever you want to call it?" And the answer, my answer to that is, "Because that's not where men are." And, the final test for me of the legitimacy of the experience is, "How well does your experience of the sacred in nature enable you to cope more effectively with the problems of mankind when you come back to the city?"

And now you see how this phases with the role of the wilderness. It's a renewal exercise and as I visualize it, it leads to a process of alternation. You go to nature for your metaphysical fix—your reassurance that there's something behind it all and it's good. You come back to where men are, to where men are messing things up, because men tend to, and you come back with a new ability to relate to your fellow man to help your fellow man relate to each other.

Willi Unsoeld

To spend a lengthy period alone in the forests or mountains, a period of coming to terms with the solitude and nonhumanity of nature is to discover who, or what, one really is—a discovery hardly possible while the community is telling you what you are, or ought to be.

Alan Watts

Life . . . is like music. Music is not designed to get to the end of itself. If this was so, one would play music as fast as possible to get to the end.

Alan Watts

Now I see the secret of the making of the best persons. It is to grow in the open air, and to eat and sleep with the earth.

Walt Whitman

The air is fragrant with summer—swamp scent—a blend of mud, algae, soapflower, and buttonbush. All around us is the sleepy music of summer swamp—the rattle of a kingfisher, the chucking of the now mostly quiet red-winged blackbirds, the banjo twang of green frogs, the buzz of cicadas starting in one red maple and picking up in another. I learned a long time ago one of the things swamps are good for is slowing summers that go by too fast.

Ted Williams

Come forth into the light of things. Let nature be your teacher.

William Wordsworth

Silence and seclusion are the secrets of success. In this modern life of activity there is only one way to separate yourself from its cease-less demands: get away from it once in a while.

Paramahansa Yogananda

After walking for days, coming home bugbitten, shins bruised, nose peeling, feet and hands swollen, I feel ablaze with life. I suspect that the canyons give me an intensified sense of living partly because I not only face the basics of living and survival, but carry them on my back. And in my head. And this intense personal responsibility gives me an overwhelming sense of freedom I know nowhere else.

Ann Zwinger
Wind in the Rock: The Canyonlands of Southeastern Utah

Women

The Rubicons which women must cross, the sex barriers which they must breech, are ultimately those that exist in their own minds.

Freda Adler

Through the years I have felt both pain and occasional anger at the attitudes of many in the established climbing community towards me and other women climbers. But when the press asks me about discrimination by men—and they frequently do—my answers have always been deliberately vague. Our achievements should speak for themselves.

Arlene Blum
Annapurna: A Woman's Place

There is more difference within the sexes than between them.

Ivy Compton-Burnett

I've never noticed that being a woman is a handicap or a plus. I am a
woman and there are men and we climb together. Sometimes I'm
stronger, sometimes they're stronger—we motivate each other.

Robyn Erbesfield

As women we must learn to become leaders in society, not just for
our own sake, but for the sake of all people. We must support and
protect our kinship with the environment for the generations to come.

China Galland

It is true that men and women as groups tend to have a shared, gen-
der-specific profile of strong and weak points. An analysis of emotional intelligence in thousands of men and women found that
women, on average, are more aware of their emotions, show more
empathy, and are more adept interpersonally. Men, on the other hand,
are more self-confident, and optimistic, adapt more easily, and handle stress better.

In general, however, there are far more similarities than
differences. Some men are as empathic as the most interpersonally
sensitive women, while some women are every bit as able to
withstand stress as the most emotionally resilient men. Indeed, on
average, looking at the overall ratings for men and women (interna-
tional group of 15,000), the strengths and weaknesses average out, so
that in terms of total emotional intelligence, there are no sex differences.

Daniel Goleman
Working with Emotional Intelligence

To be meek, patient, tactful, modest, honorable, brave, is not to be
either manly or womanly; it is to be humane.

Jane Harrison

Perhaps both men and women in America may hunger, in our material, outward, active, masculine culture, for the supposedly feminine
qualities of heart, mind and spirit—qualities which are actually neither masculine nor feminine, but simply human qualities that have

been neglected. It is growth along these lines that will make us whole, and will enable the individual to become a world to himself.

Anne Morrow Lindbergh

Women are repeatedly accused of taking things personally. I cannot see any other honest way of taking them.

Marya Mannes

On the first morning, I took them up Middle Fell Buttress: five of us, all on one rope. It was slow, cold, and boring. They climbed faster than I did, surrounded with an almost visible aura of masculine resentment. So I took them to Gwynne's Chimney on Pavey Ark, and as they struggled and sweated in that smooth cleft, sparks flying from their nails, and me waiting at the top with a taut rope and a turn round my wrist, I knew that I had won. The atmosphere—when we were all together again—was clear and relaxed.

Gwen Moffat

Sport holds a mirror to a woman's life. She learns not only how she moves, but how she feels, and thinks, and struggles, how she is tormented, triumphs, and then finds peace.

LaFerne Ellis Price

To be somebody, a woman does not have to be more like a man, but has to be more of a woman.

Sally E. Shaywitz

One of the things about equality is not just that you be treated equally to a man, but that you treat yourself equally to the way you treat a man.

Marlo Thomas

In common with many women, I felt that these Dolomites were made to suit me with their small, but excellent toe- and finger-holds, and pitches where a delicate sense of balance was the key, rather than brute force. While it helps, of course, to have tough muscles, the

prize fighter would not necessarily make a fine Dolomite climber.
But the ballet dancer might.

Miriam Underhill

Man cannot degrade women without himself falling into degradation;
he cannot elevate her without at the same time elevating himself.

Alexander Walker

Never noticed a female monkey not climbing as well as a male, have
you?

Don Whillans

I can't remember a single time that I was prevented from doing what
I wanted because I was a female, either on the rock or in the mountains.

Annie Whitehouse

End Quotes

I hate quotations. Tell me what you know.

Ralph Waldo Emerson

Not fare well, but fare forward, voyagers.

T. S. Eliot

Author Index